# HOW TO HEAL FROM TOXIC PARENTS

RACHEL STONE

Copyright © 2022 by Rachel Stone

All rights reserved.

No part of this book may be reproduced in any form or by any electronic or mechanical means, including information storage and retrieval systems, without written permission from the author, except for the use of brief quotations in a book review.

## Claim Your Freebie NOW!

Get Good At Problem Solving

Want to know the secret behind getting good at problem solving? Everyone seems to be able to do it, but you're stuck in the pile of endless to-do lists with little progress.

Ok, so how do I get my FREE book?

EASY! See the next page

Claim Your Freebie NOW

Instructions:

1. Open the camera or the QR reader application on your smartphone.
2. Point your camera at the QR code to scan the QR code.
3. A notification will pop-up on screen.
4. Click on the notification to open the website link

# Contents

| | |
|---|---|
| Introduction | ix |
| 1. WHAT IS A TOXIC PARENT? | 1 |
| Does your parent have toxic traits? | 3 |
| The child who took over parental responsibilities | 6 |
| Reverse parenting's consequences | 7 |
| Types Of Toxic Parents | 8 |
| 2. 'BUT I WASN'T BADLY ABUSED' BUT YOU STILL FEEL LIKE YOUR FAMILY DIDN'T EMBRACE YOU | 12 |
| Narcissistic wounding | 12 |
| Do you think you were inflicted early narcissistic wounds? | 14 |
| Signs of possible narcissistic wounding in the early years of parenthood | 14 |
| Self-consciousness and beliefs | 15 |
| Self-help | 19 |
| 3. HOW TO SET BOUNDARIES WITH YOUR PARENTS NOW | 22 |
| Let go of the need for approval | 23 |
| Determine tolerance limits | 25 |
| Dos and don'ts after breaking up | 26 |
| Twisted nonsense's double bind | 26 |
| Taking a look inside the canned views of family | 27 |
| Getting rid of family titles as a boundary | 28 |
| There are new routes up the mountain | 29 |
| 4. I'M A PARENT; WILL I BE TOXIC TOWARDS MY CHILDREN? | 31 |
| The advantages of this kind of self-examination | 31 |
| Recovering from early trauma | 32 |
| Build a solid personality | 33 |
| Adopt a more productive mentality and action plan | 35 |

| | |
|---|---|
| 5. SELF-STRENGTHENING TOOLS | 43 |
| Emerge from feeling broken | 43 |
| Goals for a less self-absorbed person | 53 |
| 6. Define the person you want to be | 61 |
| 7. CREATE A NEW AND BETTER YOU | 67 |
| The influence of early life events on your personality | 68 |
| Responding to your self-absorbed parent with compassion and introspection | 69 |
| Gaining strength through creative activities | 71 |
| Having a sense of purpose | 72 |
| Fairness, integrity, and collaboration | 74 |
| Become empathic in your relationships | 75 |
| A good mix of fun and responsibility | 75 |
| Positive emotional outbursts | 76 |
| Begin the process of forgiveness | 76 |
| Forgiveness | 77 |
| Conclusion | 81 |
| Feedback | 83 |

## Introduction

Our connection with our parents has a profound effect on our lives and the lives of our children and grandchildren. It is beyond the scope of this introduction and this book to discuss how main love objects influence transgenerational patterns. The desire to raise your children to be happy, healthy, self-confident, and resilient is a natural part of parenthood. Instead of being in a romantic relationship, you've found yourself in a familial situation with a selfish partner that is always nasty and aggressive. This person appears to live in a parallel universe between you and your children, easily agitated by mundane occurrences and making illogical demands, never happy with you and your family, and continuously changing the rules. Everything suddenly goes haywire, apparently for no apparent cause, in seconds. The two of you are always at odds.

Since you and your partner first met, there has been a noticeable shift in their behaviour. When you first met the person you'll be raising a child with, your relationship seemed exciting, passionate, and full of potential. There are moments when you feel like you're losing your mind because it's so different. Even though you're doing all you can to keep your relationship together, you're unsure whether it will last. Everything changes when one of your family members exhibits narcissistic or borderline personality traits. Your family's unique circumstances need a different approach to parenting and relationships. It's frustrating when you and the other parent seem to be on the same page only to have the other parent abruptly veer off course and say or do things that aren't in line with your expectations or agreement. Disputes appear out of nowhere and are often unresolved. They're extremely theatrical and upset the whole family. Although you've heard from the experts that parents must collaborate and maintain a "unified front," you're finding it difficult to do so. When the other parent seems so emotionally out of control, it may be difficult to know whether to stick by your partner or step in to protect your children from this person's abuse.

This book provides an alternative approach to parenting for your unique scenario.

People who have narcissistic or borderline personality characteristics have a very different outlook on life and deal with stress in a frequently counterproductive manner. They have misunderstood many social signs since they're excessively focused on their own viewpoint. Their expectations of their children are often selfish, inconsistent, and unconnected to the actual needs or talents of the child in question. There is a lot of confusion about what is happening and how to fix it so your family can return to the "normal" state you had hoped for.

We know how challenging it may be to raise a completely engrossed child in their distorted perception of the world. It's not easy to raise a child when you have narcissistic or borderline personality traits.

It frequently necessitates you to behave in a significantly different way from how you would normally engage with someone. When it comes to marriage and parenthood, you can't always heed experts' advice.

This book aims to show you how to help your children succeed despite the less-than-ideal family dynamics you may be dealing with. Our goal is to assist you and your children develop resilience, bravery, self-esteem, and self-compassion so that you may help them flourish and bloom into the unique and amazing individuals they were destined to be. Rather than becoming sucked into the caretaking of the other parent at the cost of your children, we want to assist you in retaining your focus on your children's healthy growth and needs. Using this book's emotional prescription, you may help your children deal with their terrible family circumstances while also ensuring your children's emotional well-being.

As a parent of a child with an emotionally unstable relationship, you struggle to maintain your composure and strength while avoiding being irrational and oppressive. Accurate perceptions and special talents are required to achieve this delicate equilibrium. To maintain your body and mind in top shape, you'll need a lot of help. You want to raise healthy, resilient children while moderating the frequently disproportionate reactions from the narcissistic or borderline parent. This is a difficult balance to strike.

Despite the difficulties, it doesn't mean that growing up with someone who has a borderline personality disorder or a narcissistic personality disorder is inevitable. Your attitude and how you manage the circumstance may profoundly affect your children's lives. Many things may be done to assist your children in comprehending what is going on, minimise hazardous relationships with an emotionally unstable parent, and improve their general development. Providing a calmer, more secure, and happier childhood for children is our objective for you so that they grow into compassionate, competent, loving, and brave adults.

# 1

## What is a toxic parent?

TOXIC PEOPLE. What are their identities?

Is it true that everyone is poisonous? No, it isn't. Not everyone is like that. There you have it, some good news.

Toxic people may be part of our own families. Our mother, father, siblings, grandparents, other relatives, and even our children may all be toxic to us.

There is no such thing as a perfect human being. We all have flaws, but imperfections are not the same as being pathological or poisonous. This includes us, as their family members, who may not see our loved ones as toxic since their toxicity isn't obvious to us. We assume that just because someone seems to be decent, it means they are. This, however, is incorrect. Appearances may be deceiving because they hide the truth underneath the surface. A toxic person's genuine character, mindset, and will are all factors in determining whether or not he or she is toxic. Consistency and persistence of manipulative conduct is the only way to see it in action.

As long as we're honest about our flaws, we're not afraid to admit them. At times we make mistakes, and we're more than happy to joke about it and apologise if required. Instead of fighting, we strive for harmony, intimacy, clarity, and personal growth.

It's fairly uncommon for people with pathological personalities to exhibit regressive behaviour, stubbornness and aggression, and vengeance. They can never be incorrect. They don't make excuses. There is no room for doubt about whether they could or should have done things differently in their minds. It's all an elaborate story of how others have mistreated them, and it's all they know.

We're dealing with people who have a sense of balance and calm when they're healthy. They are self-aware, reasonable, and calm, willing to learn from others.

A pathological person is like a two- to five-year-old in a body that's an adult. Toxic people are difficult to deal with because we're dealing with an adult who acts like a child. Our two-year-old narcissism faded away as a natural part of our maturation. Our brains have a hard time comprehending an adult's emotional response system if they are still operating from a level of self-centredness that resembles that of a child, much alone if this adult is our parent. In the same way that children make all of their choices based on their emotions, toxic people do the same. As long as they get what they want, they don't think about the repercussions. The opposite is true for those in good health, who take the time to consider the consequences of their actions before taking any action.

People with toxic personalities cannot accept the idea of others' feelings. Talking with them is difficult since they tend to be more self-referential than self-reflective. Such individuals automatically convert your tale into one about them when you tell them anything about yourself. The self-referential aspect of toxicity makes toxic individuals the greatest one-ups, name-droppers, and frauds you'll ever encounter. Without a natural back-and-forth flow, you can't have a mutually productive dialogue. When interacting with toxic people, the concept of sharing is nonexistent. Even healthy people with flaws may exhibit some of the same behaviours as toxic persons. There is a big difference between telling the truth to someone and telling the truth to someone who is a danger to themselves and others.

## Does your parent have toxic traits?

Self-absorption is characterised by a persistent and excessive concentration on oneself in almost every event. Even when their actions seem to assist others, the motivations behind the actions of self-centred individuals are almost always driven by their desires. This self-obsession is referred to as a Destructive Narcissistic Pattern (DNP).

A Destructive Narcissistic Pattern is likely to exhibit the following actions and attitudes. Look through the following descriptions to see which one best describes your parent. You don't necessarily need to have or display all of these traits for your connection with the parent to be strained by them.

Your parent's unrealistic expectations for your success, performance, and wealth signify their grandiosity. The parent is always looking to win, has little regard for others' needs, and has no concept of their boundaries.

An entitlement mentality sees others as extensions of oneself and believes that others may be manipulated and exist only to fulfil one's desires, even if those desires aren't verbalised. Others are not seen as unique persons. In the eyes of the parent, their needs are more important than those of others, and they anticipate and demand special care.

The parent lacks empathy for the effect of their critical, insulting, and devaluing words about you and others, yet expects people to be compassionate toward the parent. Parental blaming is a continual source of frustration and anguish in their household.

**Parental extensions**

Because the parent doesn't see others as distinct persons, they demand favours but don't reciprocate them. When a parent offers directions, they want them to be followed quickly and expect others to understand what they want without talking. Invading personal space and telling people what they should or shouldn't do are hallmarks of the parent's behaviour.

The impoverished self frequently complains about being

deprived, excluded, or diminished, even though there is no evidence to support this viewpoint. Self-deprecating parents will feel enraged or wounded when their children hear others agreeing with their self-deprecating remarks. To persuade others to share his or her point of view, the conceited parent will resort to personal insults.

These actions and attitudes are easy to see since the parent is likely to engage in some or all of them. There are several ways to draw attention to yourself, such as speaking out, talking a lot, entering and departing areas loudly, and making big motions.

The parent is looking for outward indicators of their child's value, superiority, and the like. Thus they encourage their child to engage in actions that seek public praise and applause. When a parent brags and extols their virtues, they're trying to get praise for their work. Insincere praises do not elicit a response from the parent, who replies with flattery of his or her own will.

Self-absorbed parents express and feel a limited range of emotions, mostly fear and anger. They use words to express their emotions, yet they are useless and hollow.

Envy is a feeling of resentment toward the success, achievements, assets, or opportunities of others that is expressed via words and actions. The parent's reaction is to feel that other people are not entitled to their love. Feelings of jealousy might trigger the impoverished self.

**Contempt**

When someone feels superior, they may treat others with contempt, assuming that they are less deserving, useful, or worthy than they are. Some examples include saying that impoverished people do not deserve help because they are not valuable or worthy of it.

Arrogance manifests as actions such as talking down to or condescending to others or displaying a sense of self-righteous superiority. It is fairly uncommon for parents to make repeated allusions to their superiority to let people know that they believe they are better than others.

The empty person regards relationships as being for personal convenience and jumps from relationship to relationship, never able to create genuine bonds. They have difficulty forming and maintaining long-term relationships, grow uncomfortable when left alone, and appear to seek or require action.

A parenting style known as "reverse parenting" is one in which the child is expected to take responsibility for his or her parents' well-being rather than the other way around. The following are examples of utterances that indicate this attitude: "If you cared about me, you'd... "I like it when you... Do you not want to be loved by me?" 'You're so kind to me when you...' It hurts my feelings when you let me down. "Why can't you do what I ask of you?"

When a parent insists that their child thrive in sports and academics or demonstrate other abilities, the child's reflected glory is a source of pride for the parent. The parent will be dissatisfied if the child isn't a huge success. The child's desires are also ignored or treated with indifference by the parent.

No regard for a child as a person with his or her values and wants is shown by parents who treat their children as an extension of themselves. As a result, they refuse to accept any dissent or criticism and blame their child for any perceived flaws and shortcomings.

People who engage in this kind of conduct and attitude also show signs of a lack of empathy for other people. As a result, other people are seen as being exploited for the parent's benefit, including taking advantage of others, manipulating others, and claiming credit that has not been earned.

Reading through these descriptions with your parent in mind, you've undoubtedly recognised that your parent possessed some of these qualities but not all. If, on the other hand, you have reason to suspect that your parent exhibits several traits indicative of self-centredness, continue reading to learn more about the influence this may have had on your development as a child and the effects it may still be having on you now. There are many sorts of self-absorbed parents mentioned in this section, and your parent's conduct and attitudes may reflect one of these types. However, it's vital to remember that these classifications and categories aren't absolutes. They are used to facilitate conversation.

## The child who took over parental responsibilities

It's not only that these parents are self-absorbed, but that they also believe that their children are accountable for their well-being, rather than the other way around. All or almost all of the following things happen to children who grow up in these kinds of environments:

- The adult child is still a part of the parent's life.
- Even as an adult, the child is still subject to parental authority.
- Even as an adult, the child must always satisfy their parents' expectations, even if they have their own needs and expectations of themselves.
- The child must be able to foresee and meet the demands and wishes of the parents.
- The child must pay attention to and respect the parent at all times.
- As a result, the child is expected to give up their well-being to care for the older relative.
- The child must be empathetic to the parent but not expect or demand empathy.
- The parent's image will be tarnished if the child makes mistakes or displays bad judgment.
- Children are obligated to stop what they are doing if their parent tells them to, even if they don't want to.
- The child must never exercise independence or autonomy.

Self-absorbed parents' conduct and attitudes are passed down to their children early, preventing them from developing as unique people who can make their own decisions. Take a look at the following and see whether it describes your current state of mind, emotions, or outlook:

- Do you have a hard time establishing long-lasting connections with people you care about?

- Is it difficult to tell when people attempt to get you to do things that are not in your best interests?
- Do you have trouble expressing a broad range of feelings to others?
- Do you have trouble letting go of other people's feelings?
- Do you find yourself getting caught up in the feelings of others around you?
- Do you take other people's words and actions personally?
- Do you struggle with unpleasant emotions like anger or resentment?
- Does it cause you to be on edge and anxious to please other people?
- Do you have a hard time making choices because you're afraid of making a bad one?
- Do you ever wonder why some people appear to be happier and more content than you are in their lives?

If you identified with several of these, you might be experiencing long-lasting negative impacts that stem from having grown up with a toxic, narcissistic parent. The way you behave, feel, and interact now may reflect how you were raised to act and relate with your narcissistic parent.

## Reverse parenting's consequences

The following explains how the adult child's emotional vulnerability may be affected by reverse parenting. As you read on, attempt to assess how often or powerfully you feel what is mentioned.

Increased emotional sensitivity is one of the most problematic and long-lasting side effects of reverse parenting. An emotional vulnerability is the propensity to "catch" others' sentiments (typically unpleasant feelings) and then find yourself unable to get rid of them quickly. As a child, your psychological boundary strength was lacking, making it difficult for you to distinguish between the feelings you can tolerate and those you should reject. Does it occur to you to perform any or all of these things?

- Constantly observe people and attempt to identify what they are experiencing so that you may help them if they seem to be in need or suffering.
- When others are in difficulty, you get disturbed and find it difficult to let go of those sentiments.
- Feel the need to win the approval of others constantly.
- Make an effort to look out for the welfare or emotional well-being of others, even if they are mature adults who can take care of themselves.
- Never let go of the sensations that cause you to be on edge or perhaps inconsolable.
- Feel terrified of any indications of confrontation, even if you are not participating.
- You can only feel optimistic or cheerful if those around you are also.

If you discovered that several of these characteristics applied to you, the following section might help you understand what is going on. You may be suffering from painful emotions because of your emotional sensitivity and psychological boundary strength.

## Types Of Toxic Parents

As a child, it might be difficult to understand why your parent exhibits certain toxic behaviours but not others. **Needy, prickly, deceitful,** and **grandstanding** parents may all be lumped together for this debate. For each, we'll provide a brief overview, a rundown of typical actions, and examples of what a child who is either obedient or rebellious would say in response to each.

**Needy**

Needy, toxic parents, may seem to others as attentive and caring. This parent is particularly concerned about their child's well-being and wants to be recognised for their efforts. Specifically, this need for recognition is indicative of a self-obsessed mindset. The child and others must be grateful and appreciative of this parent's actions.

The child is not cared for purely altruistically; instead, the child is expected to "pay" for the care with emotional currency. For example, a toddler asserting his or her growing independence might result in anger towards the parent or demanding control and management over the child if the parent feels their efforts aren't appreciated (for example, by overprotecting). Everyone knows how much effort, sacrifice, and attention this parent puts in to ensure that no one will forget about it.

Symptoms of a needy, toxic parent include clutching, over nurturing, and an overzealous sense of duty. In this case, parents could exaggerate their sacrifices, whine excessively about various issues, and show signs of anxiety when left alone. They constantly bug you to find out what you're thinking, feeling, and believing, never forget an offence and are vulnerable to being wounded since they are very sensitive to criticism. Parents who lack empathy may seem to sympathise, but this is not the case.

**Prickly**

Prickly toxic parents are very demanding and want immediate and exact compliance with their requirements, whether or not they have been vocally communicated. Those around them are expected to "do the right thing," to "do it correctly," without ever getting an appropriate explanation from the parent of what "right" means to the child. This parent may also be very sensitive, picking up on feelings of disapproval, criticism, and blame in almost everything said or done, regardless of the intended meaning. As a result, children who have parents like this are continually on edge, watchful of their words and actions, and persistent in their attempts to "get it right" or retreat emotionally or physically.

This kind of parent displays a variety of actions and attitudes, such as never being satisfied, being very judgmental of others, and demanding that everything must be done according to the parent's specifications. Demanding perfection, blaming the child and others for their discomfort, and making degrading or devaluing statements to or about the child and others, these parents take offence readily at what the parent perceives as criticism.

## Deceitful

Conniving toxic parents are constantly positioning themselves for victory, coming out on top, and ensuring that all others recognise that they are inferior. Almost every element of their lives, including their children, is governed by this principle. These parents would lie, cheat, distort, and mislead to attain their aims. Others, even their children, are considered fair game for manipulation and exploitation. So-called "controlling" parents are good at gauging their children's feelings to exploit them. In adulthood, their progeny may distrust others' motivations or tend to get into partnerships where they are coerced into doing things against their will or their best interests.

Being manipulative, having a must-win-at-any-cost mindset, and a readiness to lie, cheat, mislead, and distort to acquire what they want—sometimes merely to see whether others would be conned—are all characteristics of the cunning parent. These parents may resort to coercion, seduction, or even ingratiation to get their way. A thief always looks for the best opportunity or an advantage over everyone else, whether it's taking advantage of someone else, dismissing someone else as inferior, or being vengeful. Assuming that everyone would do what they want without question and that everyone else is exactly like them, this sort of parent must get their licks in before anybody else.

## Grandstanding

This refers to a parent who is "always on stage," "playing to the audience," and "bigger than life." Everyone else has a function to play in this parent's universe that must be submissive to the parent's self-perception. Parents' children are seen as extensions of their parents, and they exist to improve and increase the areas in which their parents might be praised, gain attention, be better than others, and the like. There must be no failure for the child, and if there is, that success is seen as a direct result of the parent's efforts. The impacts on these children may create someone shy, cautious, constantly seeking attention and appreciation, or someone who acts out to attain the same results that their parents do.

Flamboyant and theatrical conduct, continual boasting and bragging, and exaggerating one's triumphs and afflictions are all characteristics of this sort of toxic parent. This kind of parent is always on the go, from one relationship or endeavour to the next, and it seems that they never stop. It's not uncommon for them to exaggerate their skills, capacities, and talents; they also dislike others who receive the attention for doing better. They may also be very invasive and disdainful of others' psychological boundaries, property, or personal space and take control of everything.

## 2

# 'But I wasn't badly abused' but you still feel like your family didn't embrace you

A CHILD's adult life is still influenced by the early acts and words of his or her parents. Without the child's knowledge or awareness, these behaviours and messages were powerfully absorbed into the child's life. They shape the kid's self-worth and continue to do so as an adult, often in ways, the child isn't even aware of. During childhood, their parents' acts and words caused profound scars that have not yet healed. Here is an explanation of how early parental words and acts may continue to influence someone as an adult and the significance these early injuries have in the adult's self-perception.

### Narcissistic wounding

An injury to the fundamental self is a narcissistic wound. The signals a person gets suggest that they are fatally defective, unvalued, or of little value cause these wounds. Even before a child has the vocabulary to verbalise what they've absorbed due to their experiences, they might be wounded. A parent's handling and response to a baby or child might convey a message about the parent's perspective on the child since parents typically provide care for the youngster. A child's narcissistic injury might last a long time if he or she is ignored as an infant or youngster. In the long run, this unfavourable view of oneself as an adult might be reinforced by subsequent wounds.

No matter how much time has passed, you may not yet be aware of how your early life experiences continue to shape who you are now, how you interact with others and even some of the things you do. There was a complex interaction between your parent's reactions to you, the signals they were sending you about who you are, and the personality and responses you had towards them that led to the injuries and lack of development you are now struggling with.

How your parents responded to you as a growing child had a significant impact on your sense of self-worth. Parents' empathetic awareness and responsiveness aid the development of a child's self-esteem. Due to your parent's self-obsessiveness may not have received the empathy that would have made you feel valued, treasured, and loved. While empathy or its absence may not affect all of your self-esteem, you may still be suffering from significant self-esteem problems.

Messages from parents, conscious and unconscious, are assimilated into the child's psyche and acted upon by the child, generally in unconscious ways. You are unaware of how these signals influence your ideas and emotions about your core inner self, your attitudes and reactions to and about other people, and your actions. These statements from parents have a profound impact. When you were a child, you got messages from your parents about how much they valued you, what you looked like, how smart you were, what you did for the family, how much you were loved, and other things. It's easy to see the significance of parental signals and the long-term consequences.

Each individual is unique, with their personality and reaction to their parents. Although some of these may be generalised, the effects are unique to each individual. When it comes to self-esteem, everyone who grows up in an environment where their parents are self-absorbed is likely to suffer lasting damage to their self-esteem. This chapter will examine some of the probable implications that parental signals may have on the adult offspring of self-absorbed parents.

### Do you think you were inflicted early narcissistic wounds?

It is difficult to comprehend how narcissistic wounding occurs when you have not yet recovered from harm to your core self. Until you could retain memories in the language, you use and understand today, an injury that occurred to your child as a baby or toddler may have gone unremembered. Indirect, concealed, and camouflaged effects of these early traumas might still be felt. While some may have difficulty starting and maintaining long-term relationships, others may find that they are easily hurt by criticism. The effects of childhood trauma may linger on into adulthood, affecting your self-esteem and causing you to engage in self-destructive behaviour.

You must understand yourself and any views about your worth and value that you may have developed due to your childhood wounds. For example, do you believe that you must have deep and personal relationships to feel loved, competent, valuable, secure, and respected? Do you keep getting into relationships that aren't fulfilling in the hopes of finding the one person who can offer you the affection you truly desire? Consequently, if this is the case, you may want to think about how your present activities may be a result of your deep-seated needs nurtured by your self-absorbed parent's defective parenting.

### Signs of possible narcissistic wounding in the early years of parenthood

The following are some signs that a person is suffering from narcissistic wounding. Think about whether any of the following phrases resonate with you regularly or if they're prompted in situations when you've experienced discomfort.

- I am defective, and if people can see my shortcomings, they will not like or approve of me.
- I am not living according to my standards and principles because I allow people to control me.
- I cannot keep myself from doing what others want me to do.

- I believe that most individuals are more competent, skilled, and sufficient than I am.
- I live in constant terror of being exposed for who I am, and I'm afraid that I'll be ruined if that occurs.
- I cannot survive if others do not like and accept me.
- I can't stop people from ruining or leaving me.

When you read these self-statements, how accurate do they feel? The following are examples of additional signals:

- You're in a relationship that's in danger of falling apart.
- You're not happy with many things about yourself, including the way you look.
- You are never or seldom content or think you have enough.
- You're always doubting your abilities.
- You can never rely on anybody else.
- You lack purpose or significance in your life.
- You are always criticising yourself.

If two or more of these phrases connect with you, you may have been narcissistically wounded as a child. Here are some ideas on how you may better understand how this early wounded has affected you and how you might begin the healing process.

### Self-consciousness and beliefs

People's negative self-statements are caused by their views about their core inner self, not by what someone else says or does. What others say or do would not arouse such unpleasant emotions if you did not have these self-limiting ideas about your core inner being. You are aware of some of the beliefs you have. Those that are repressed just below the level of consciousness, but that may erupt at any moment, and those buried deep in your unconscious, and the only way you have any idea that they exist is via your responses. It's possible to deny that you have these self-defeating ideas consciously, but if you didn't, you wouldn't be experiencing the distress that comes with them. Your task is to comprehend and modify your negative, defeating, and non-constructive thoughts about yourself.

The following are examples of self-statements that may be causing your injuries:

- I need the approval of others to live. As a person, it is uplifting to know that you have the support of others. Having their seal of approval means that you can rest easy, knowing that you will not be abandoned or damaged. Even though this may look excessive, the anxiety underlying the desire for acceptance is fundamental, even if it's seldom stated as dread. Fear of rejection and a need for acceptance permeates every human being.

- With adequate support from family and other key individuals in your early childhood, you can have enough self-confidence to feel that you're acceptable, and others will support and encourage you. A fundamental level of approbation signifies that someone loved and accepted you for who you were.

- I feel obligated to be flawless. The feeling that you are responsible for being flawless might bring you considerable suffering since you can never be completely pleased with your core inner nature. You're never quite good enough, and external validation isn't enough to help you enjoy or accept your imperfections. When you're obsessed with being flawless, you may even expect that people in your life do the same. Your relationships may suffer due to your tendency to extend yourself to others.

- I must always take care of other people. Being worried for others is admirable, but it is unreasonable to take responsibility for everyone, to be too protective, to not accept and think that others are capable of self-care, to be intrusive with your actions of caring, to demand that others accept these activities or to feel guilty or humiliated when others are in pain. Signs of over-responsibility and a lack of understanding of others' needs for independence and autonomy may be seen in these behaviours. In these situations, you are probably unwittingly striving to satisfy unfulfilled expectations from your upbringing. If any of these expectations are not met, you feel guilty or humiliated, and you become nervous.

- The needs of other individuals are more essential than my own. You may have learned early on that your own needs were less important than those of others. Lack of empathy from a parent or caregiver, neglect, blaming, criticism, inability to accept and respect you as you are, and other similar events may have influenced your idea that others' needs should come before your own. It will be tough for you to strike a suitable balance between self-care and the urge to care for others to overcome this idea.

- I am so imperfect that I will never be better. When you feel that your flaws are so great that you will never improve, despair, hopelessness, and helplessness are likely to follow. It is possible to get depressed due to these sentiments, which arise when you are wounded or embarrassed. What seems to be a never-ending stream of insults, blame, and other unpleasant statements may be demoralising. You're stumped as to why you can't seem to "get it right" while others appear to be able to.

- I can't stay alive if no one takes care of me. Emotional and psychological caretaking is often associated with the idea that someone else should be responsible for one's well-being. Adults who need physical care are excluded from this conversation since they have the same beliefs as the rest of us. Intimacy and closeness are at the heart of what we're discussing. Having such a notion about oneself may cause a lot of pain and make you feel like you've been abandoned. As a result, you may find yourself in unhealthy situations, doing things you don't want to and allowing yourself to be demeaned or devalued in the process.

- I can't let people see the true me because they'll reject me. There are elements of yourself that you are aware of but want to keep concealed from others because you worry or anticipate that they would reject you if they become aware of that aspect of yourself. Is that aspect of your inner self what you consider to be the "true" you? Even the tiniest hint that someone is aware of your true self may be traumatic because you fear it will lead to your rejection.

- I am not as competent, clever, or capable as others. When you believe that you fall short of the standards set by others, you put yourself at risk of more damage and harm to your self-esteem, as you are continually reminded that others have more money, more education, more skill, a better physical appearance, a higher social position, etc. Furthermore, every mistake you make strengthens your negative self-perception of your true nature. It may be quite hurtful to receive comments or statements from others that seem to concentrate on your shortcomings and negative aspects, which might reinforce your negative ideas. You can keep yourself in a condition of perpetual pain.

- I never seem to receive what I want or need. You lack self-efficacy if you believe that you will never acquire what you desire or need. It's possible that this notion was implanted in your mind as a child due to your parents' lack of concern for your well-being, delay, neglect, or outright disregard for you.

## Self-help

You may be putting yourself at risk in light of everything you've just learned. This means that if you are hurting, you don't necessarily have to suffer as much, you don't have to let what others say or do become criticism or blame, and you don't have a strong enough self to be self-reflective and not disgraced by anything. A strong feeling of self-worth, confidence, and self-efficacy may be developed and strengthened by focusing on your core inner self. If you've been more conscious of your self-defeating habits and attitudes and attempted some of the self-affirmations in this chapter, you've already started the process.

You may also make certain perceptual adjustments that will be beneficial. As a result, you shift your perspective from self-defeating to one that is more constructive, rational, and reasonable. Making these mental shifts doesn't mean you're giving up the excellent aspects of yourself; rather, you're strengthening and honing them while minimising your feelings of shame, guilt, fear, inadequacy, and other negative self-talk. Each recommended perceptual change should be read carefully and reflected upon.

**Develop a healthier core self**

In the first part of the chapter, you learned how your early experiences with your self-absorbed parent may have influenced your present beliefs, attitudes, and actions, and how they may be hurting your self-esteem, view of yourself, and even your relationships. Further ideas are offered in the succeeding sections to understand yourself and others better and establish a healthy core self. Even though you may have many good parts of your core self, it's possible that you don't feel like the person you want to be in total. Knowing how these events are affecting you now can help you overcome some of the negative impacts of your self-absorbed parent's actions and attitudes.

Work to become the person you want to be so that your core inner self is confident, successful, and sufficient. This is the most beneficial thing you can do for yourself. The following features need to be established or improved to achieve this goal:

**Sense and purpose**

Give your life, job, and the people you interact with a sense of direction and meaning. Meaning and purpose might alter throughout a person's life, but they must remain constant.

**Show compassion**

Make a point of being nice and selfless every day. You're practising altruism when you give without expecting a return or reward. Giving to others is an act of selflessness. Everyday benevolence is beneficial to both the recipient and the giver.

**Improve your ability to empathise**

Work to improve your ability to react and relate in an empathetic way. Empathy is the ability to enter another person's world and experience what they feel without losing sight of who you are as a unique individual. This is when the other people's emotions do not overwhelm you. Empathy can be expressed without relying on profound empathy, although this isn't always achievable. An important part of empathy is recognising the other person's feelings while not necessarily experiencing them yourself and then verbalising those feelings to the other person. The benefits of recognising and appreciating the sentiments of others are enormous.

**Strengthen your body and mind**

Build up your toughness and tenacity. Adversity is a part of life, but you don't have to give in to it if you don't want to. When you're down, you get back up and try again or choose another path.

**Emotional control is key**

When dealing with a self-absorbed parent, it's important to keep your emotions in check. You'll be more successful with your self-absorbed parent and other people. You won't experience the aftereffects of these unpleasant feelings if you can control and limit your difficult and often overwhelming emotions.

**Let go of the past**

Instead of condemning yourself for not being perfect or better, learn to accept your faults and failures and move on. Self-blame, shame and guilt, and other unpleasant sentiments about yourself might stem from bad signals you received from your parents while growing up. This book's discussions and exercises will help you better know how to forgive yourself, let go of unpleasant ideas and emotions, and replace them with more lasting and gratifying ones. The point here isn't to imply that you shouldn't attempt to remove or lessen errors, but it's better if you don't obsess over them and damage your self-esteem.

Healthy self-development and healing depend on these qualities in one's core. With these pieces in place, you'll be able to handle yourself more effectively during conversations with your self-absorbed parent.

## 3

## How to set boundaries with your parents now

PERSONAL BOUNDARIES ARE BASIC GUIDELINES, norms, or restrictions you create to establish acceptable, safe, and unrestricted ways for people to act while related to you. They outline how you will react when or if someone breaks those limitations. When it comes to creating limits, anybody and everyone but our families are granted authority to do so. What's the point of this? What kind of exception would you make for people you consider to be "family"?

When you set boundaries on family members as an adult, our wider culture tells us that we are unkind to individuals we grew up with or those who raised us. Messages like these lead to your bad habit of not seeking to see whether the other players engaged in your present life are to blame for any mishaps. Instead, you might conduct a reflexive, critical, and ruthless self-examination in search of areas of weakness. Because you were raised without boundaries, you may not have considered that someone else may be to blame.

On the other hand, solid boundaries will make it easier to break links and keep your distance. Physical barriers keep good things out, and bad things are kept in. If you don't set clear emotional boundaries with your family, it's easy for such limits to become muddled, which may be particularly problematic when dealing with close family members. It's important to keep your sentiments separate from those of others. Boundaries you set for your family may make them feel belittled. To avoid violating boundaries, do not take responsibility for their emotions, allow them to blame you for their issues, abandon your own needs to satisfy them, or assume responsibility for their problems yourself. How can you tell where to draw the line? Listening to what you have to say. To know what you can and cannot endure, you must assess your boundaries. You don't break off links with your family because you're heartless, callous, or lacking in empathy—quite the contrary. You set boundaries because you care about your wounds and the safety of others.

By establishing clear boundaries with your toxic family members, you open yourself up to the healing and success you seek. People whose families have been poisoned may freely be joyful, true to who they are, and express their thoughts without fear of retribution from those they love. Everything in your life should have been like this for you. When it comes to cutting connections with your family, finding support might be tough since many people don't understand why you're doing it. However, you do not need to gain the approval of others to have the freedom to do what is best for you.

### Let go of the need for approval

Changing your life is usually the most difficult move you make. Step one is breaking relations with your family because you realise that healing cannot take place in the same toxic atmosphere. Cutting ties isn't a prank. It takes a lot of guts to accomplish something like this. It's a difficult and painful process because, no matter your age, you want to feel that you have the consent and support required to withdraw yourself from your family. Many individuals in our society are unwilling to provide this consent. Boundaries by Cloud and Townsend argue that you need the assistance of people closest to you to define and keep your boundaries for the following reasons:

- You have a deep-seated need to be loved and accepted. Relationships are difficult to establish and maintain, and people will go through great pains. Many of us are shackled to our dysfunctional families for years because we are afraid to be alone. Those contemplating such a decision have little to no help in the form of churches, therapists, or even friends. Even while you rightly believe that if everything is going well, people will support you, your lack of support just makes it more difficult to build and keep the boundaries necessary to liberate yourself.

- You need help dispelling the myth that you'll lose the affection you've always cherished if you create healthy boundaries with your family.

As a result of having well-defined boundaries, you'll find yourself in a difficult situation: It is unlikely that you will find much support from those who believe in the goodness of all people if you decide to pursue this step. The result is a constant battle with others' attempts to cure your issue for you so that they may feel at ease with your family dynamic. This brings up the question: Why is it necessary for others to be at ease with your family dynamic? Just because they don't like the idea of anything not fitting neatly into a box? Some individuals may offer to assist you in restoring their image of peace between you and your family members, not so you can be comfortable, but so they can. You don't need anybody else's consent or permission to set healthy boundaries around your actions to protect yourself. Permission to act comes solely from the impulses that urge you to protect yourself.

I advise you to pay more attention to your thoughts and feelings than those of others. Let go of the desire for approval to set the boundaries you know you need a difficult but necessary discipline. Because it is your life to live, not anybody else's, the permission you give yourself is more than enough. Your loved ones will not appreciate the limitations you place on them. Because they don't examine the nature of your connection with them, they believe they are entitled to have their way with your relationship with them. You have to determine what is acceptable and unacceptable in your life.

## Determine tolerance limits

The most valuable gift that boundaries provide is a clear distinction between where one person ends and the other begins. Your instincts will warn you of an unacceptable invasion of your personal/emotional space when you are sufficiently far from the other. To prevent more misunderstanding or harm, you need to set a boundary to preserve that holy area of your life. If you accept responsibility for the wrong things and people because of unhealthy connections, you're living in the wrong place. Boundaries, on the other hand, are not always so clear-cut. There must be some wiggle space in the boundaries. You may use the following guidelines to determine a person's tolerance levels while establishing boundaries:

Decide what you will and will not tolerate: You must decide your tolerance levels.

**Pay attention to sentiments of resentment**

These feelings indicate when someone has imposed their expectations, beliefs, demands, or values on you without your agreement or interest.

There are two ways to create boundaries: you can either be very explicit or very quiet. First, inform the individual or persons who violate your boundaries how you feel when they participate in actions that make you uncomfortable. This approach is most effective when both parties are willing to provide and receive feedback. Silence is often the most effective strategy when dealing with toxic people who will hold everything you do or say against you.

The main dangers of established borders of tolerance are fear and guilt: To have complete control over your own life, you must speak up for what is right and fight for what you believe in.

**Respect your feelings**

The more you learn about yourself and your feelings, the more you'll be able to create healthy boundaries for yourself and your well-being.

**Seek advice**

Whether you're unsure if you're overreacting to a person's words or actions or if you think you may have misunderstood something, don't be afraid to ask for help.

The art and science of establishing boundaries is a delicate balancing act. You must communicate openly with your family members what your needs and boundaries are while also adjusting your communication to garner the least backlash.

Start by creating minor boundaries like "Unfortunately, this week is quite hectic and I will not be able to talk." Gaining confidence to establish more major restrictions such as, "If you treat me badly I will withdraw myself from your presence," will come when you achieve little accomplishments. Unprotected living results in a life of paranoia, loneliness, and fear that shrinks you terribly from your true potential. Emotional strength can only be gained by setting boundaries. Setting boundaries may seem like a bad thing, but it's important to get through any negative feelings you may have about it.

## Dos and don'ts after breaking up

Once the links that bind you have been broken, it is imperative that you look after your well-being. Responding to family members' attempts to contact you (whether by phone, email, or other means) should be avoided. Your family will most likely call you if there is an emergency (we'll get into this issue in more depth). Don't be afraid to answer such phone calls, but be sure to tell the individual who contacted you about your family's boundaries. For their care and the information they have provided, thank them. That's it. Take care of yourself first and foremost, and only you and those closest to you need to remain faithful after severing relations.

## Twisted nonsense's double bind

When you attempt to explain to people why you believe you had no other alternative, things become a little more complicated. Even when people project their sometimes absurd arguments for why you've made the incorrect choice onto you, you must dig deep and believe in your decision-making abilities. If you have severed relations with a family member or close friend, you may find yourself dealing with people who have no idea how to deal with toxicity but still want to repair things. The fixers become irritated when you stick to your guns and refuse to bend to their demands. This causes others to misinterpret your intransigence and unwillingness to forgive, and the projection starts. They naively assume that reuniting with your family will cease the abuse. What does it mean for you? Back to the drawing board.

This mind-bogglingly crazy loop of twisted gibberish is certain to test your sanity and emotions. Fixers don't realise that if you've chosen to break up with someone, you've already gone through the pain and asked all the necessary questions. In situations where parents or older family members set no-contact boundaries with their adult children or younger family members, such as nieces or grandkids. I often wonder why the younger person is seen as unreasonable while parents or older family members who set boundaries based on the lack of respect they receive from the younger person are viewed as good parents and aunts, unreasonably reasonable. This doesn't make any sense at all.

This sort of blatant hypocrisy may come back to haunt you in the wake of your experience in defining "family" and the dynamics of family life. When confronted with hypocrites, you'll need to investigate this hypocrisy so that you may work through the confusion and remain steadfast in your belief in the reality of your own experience.

## Taking a look inside the canned views of family

Society's preconceived notions about family may have devastating effects on individuals who are brave enough to establish boundaries with those who abuse them. We can see, when seen objectively, how difficult it is for others to accept your choice since they don't want to be seen as people who don't respect family or believe they do. Because of the widespread apprehension about this subject, survivors have an uphill struggle in their quest for recognition. What a terrible home atmosphere you must have had if you were prepared to fight this struggle and hold strong in the face of such a clear lack of approval to stay away from your family. However, for some reason, the message isn't getting over. This illustrates how difficult it is to get people to understand the importance of family and why so many people stay victims of predatory family members' manipulation and exploitation.

The bottom line is that our actions have repercussions. In the end, whatever a person does has an equal and opposite effect. In Boundaries, Cloud and Townsend demonstrate the ramifications of family members who disobey the law of cause and effect. The law of cause and effect states that anybody who intentionally harms another will face serious repercussions. Rescue or protection from the natural consequences of someone's actions is a choice that reduces their agency. The inevitable repercussions of their actions will be met by those in your family who abuse and manipulate your emotions. What will happen to them as a result of their mistreatment? It was the end of a relationship.

A loving and accepting family is a family that can accept each other's differences in a spirit of mutual respect, with each member able to embrace their uniqueness in a spirit of openness and tolerance. There's no way you're used to living in this setting. Because of this, you don't have to feel bad about disciplining your emotionally abusive family members. You can't teach kids anything if you don't allow them to face the repercussions of their actions.

## Getting rid of family titles as a boundary

Accepting that my toxic family members are simply individuals and not authorities was one of the most important boundaries I created and one that may be beneficial and therapeutic for you. Parents and elder relatives (siblings, aunts, uncles, grandparents, cousins) have the biggest influence on your life as a youngster. Not necessarily because they have earned it, but because they are the most important part of who you are. They've grown in stature and maturity and can now support themselves independently. Follow their lead and carry out their instructions. You look up to them; you want their affection, acceptance, support, advice, time, love, and attention. You emulate them. Be silent and refrain from making any noise. Do not question or challenge their authority. Regardless of what people say, it's all good. You do all to show them that you are doing everything you can to satisfy their expectations and make them proud of you.

However, if you are living under their roof, these regulations apply. I'll never forget when I realised my mother, father, and sister were no longer my family. After a long period of suffering their abuse and a particularly heinous incident, it became evident that they were nothing more than individuals to me. You give people status and authority in your life by addressing them with titles like "mother, father," "sister," "brother," etc. You had no option but to follow in their footsteps in the beginning.

You may not be able to divorce your family legally, but you may divorce them emotionally once you reach maturity. The moment I realised how nasty my family members might be caused me to stop addressing them by their family titles. Since then, I've only used their given names while addressing them. My life has improved greatly due to this, and I hope the same for you.

This basic line of demarcation can help you remember that your family members are just like any other human being. The more you accept them as they are, the easier it will be for you. No longer giving them names and positions they formerly had that their abuse and manipulation ruined is acceptable if they are no longer in your family, leadership, or related roles. Harry Potter's mentor, Albus Dumbledore, famously said, "Call him Voldemort. When referring to anything, call it by its appropriate name. An object is more frightening when it has a fearful name.

### There are new routes up the mountain

When faced with a difficult emotional circumstance, most individuals opt to avoid rather than take action. For many years, my family and I engaged in this activity together. I propose that we challenge our inclination to avoid confrontation and look for new paths up the mountain so that we might enjoy a more beautiful top with expansive vistas of new possibilities. To reach this peak, you must ask yourself: Will avoiding the end of an abusive relationship help me get there? In the end, it won't happen. You must do what is best for your general well-being at some time if you want to be healthy and happy. Realise that you don't have to live your life as a timid pleaser terrified of disagreement just because you can't face the truth. People and situations that have been ruining you are tethered to your fear. It takes a lot of guts to go against the grain. Going against the strongly established concept that "family is important" demands a significant degree of self-regard. For some people, family is everything, but not for everyone. Those in the latter category deserve as much praise for their courage in fleeing their dysfunctional families as we do for honouring and remaining close to us.

Reflect on how much more powerful you would feel if you were no longer tied to the opinions of others. Make a list of the things you can do to protect yourself better.

You'll benefit from this self-confidence in the long run. "An eye for an eye and a tooth for a tooth" is a common behavioural paradigm in dysfunctional families. As a result, your family will want vengeance if anything horrible occurs. When your toxic family rejects you because you fail to respond to their abuses and manipulations, they sever the first links between you and your family. The bonds are severed only when you stand up for yourself and make the self-respecting choice that it is no longer your obligation to repair the harm that was not committed by you and then opt to remain quiet. People who have been mentally abused choose to retaliate against their victims rather than restore their relationships. In the coming chapters, I'll detail how to deal with their attempts. Until you get to a place where it doesn't matter whether others believe and understand you, this boundary work is worthwhile because it gets you to a position where you can defend yourself from the predatory individuals in your life without worrying about what other people think.

# 4

## I'm a parent; will I be toxic towards my children?

INJURIES TO A CHILD'S growing self-inflicted during infancy may have long-term detrimental consequences as the child grows and develops into an adult. There are indirect repercussions of childhood trauma on adults' beliefs, emotions, and behaviour. Many of these injuries are buried in memories that cannot be retrieved because they were not stored understandably after language development. Somehow, this is similar to data saved in an early computer language that modern systems cannot access because they lack the old software.

These ideas and emotions may come from childhood trauma, and this chapter focuses on recognising and understanding some of these thoughts and feelings. This section will look at the beliefs and sentiments that have stayed with you throughout your life and inhibit you from becoming a more self-aware adult.

### The advantages of this kind of self-examination

When it comes to self-discovery, it's not always easy. When you think about how you were harmed as a kid, it might cause much pain. You may wish to take a break from reading if you begin to feel anxious and return to the investigation later. Persevering in the face of discomfort may have several advantages for your personal growth, development, relationships, and overall well-being.

Improving one's core inner self has the following advantages:

- As your self-esteem and self-confidence grow, so does your public image.
- As a result, you cultivate and sustain more meaningful, productive, rewarding, and long-lasting interpersonal connections.
- Your self-absorbed parent will not inflict any more harm on you.
- Stress and bad sentiments are lessened generally, but notably in your relationship with your parent.
- As a result, you experience an increase in emotional stability and self-awareness.
- Non-conscious or unconscious erroneous views about yourself reduce the likelihood that you would be re-injured by your parent or others.

We'll also start looking at a method for dealing with the more severe sentiments you have about traumatic experiences in your past. Understandably, you want to dwell on what happened to you and its injustice, but those events are in the past, and there's nothing we can do about them. To help you, we must concentrate on how you may heal yourself and stimulate good development, and attain a more gratifying self-perception. Using this technique, you may take charge, become more productive, and better comprehend your responsibility for what occurs to you, starting now and going forward.

## Recovering from early trauma

This part discusses several fundamental assumptions that may influence your present ideas, feelings, attitudes, and behaviours unknowingly and adversely. Additionally, there is a justification for establishing a stronger and more unified fundamental inner self, how to adjust unproductive attitudes and actions, and how you may be contributing to future harm to yourself.

**Preliminary insights**

What occurred to you and how it has and continues to affect you is largely based on the following assumptions:

- Early traumas, particularly those perpetrated by your self-absorbed father, were damaging to your core personality.
- Your self-perception is shaped by the past experiences and connections you've had.
- It is difficult to let go of the unpleasant and deep sensations associated with these traumatic situations.
- You can't go back and undo the events that have occurred to you.
- You can't rely on others to change your bad sentiments, no matter how good-hearted they are or how much they care about you.
- Other people's apologies would not reduce your unfavourable sentiments.
- Your emotions and perspectives on the events and persons involved haven't changed.
- You're trying to get rid of the unpleasant sensations you're having.

A key component in recovering from childhood trauma is developing a strong sense of self-worth. You are less likely to be hurt again by your selfish parents' words and actions and less likely to feel lonely or alienated. Reflect on if your parent's toxic behaviour influences your behaviour and views.

## Build a solid personality

You will be able to let go of some of the long-term pains caused by your self-absorbed parent if you have a strong and coherent self.

This does not mean that you won't ever be wounded again, but it will lower the frequency and severity of your bad sentiments and help you to more easily let go of whatever unpleasant feelings you may have had in the past. Your physical and mental well-being will improve, as will the quality of your relationships.

A strong and coherent self will enable you to perform the following:

- Personalising what others say or do may generate shame, remorse, and more pain; therefore, avoid doing so.
- Reduce the frequency with which you experience wrath and fear by making more accurate assessments of external dangers to yourself.
- You may lessen your tendency to identify with or behave by the projected identity by recognising when someone else is displacing or projecting what they find personally undesirable onto you and then rejecting that displacement or projection.
- Distress may be alleviated by letting go of little irritations and not allowing them to accumulate.
- Accept your flaws and recognise that you have the power to improve on the things you do well while letting go of the things you wish you could alter.
- When you're content with yourself and others, it's easier to establish and sustain long-lasting friendships and romantic partnerships.
- Empathise with people in ways that are sincere, warm, and sincere.

When it comes to addressing and healing previous wounds, a big part of the process is developing your inner self further to be less vulnerable to narcissistic injury. So that you are more protected, solidly anchored, suitably guarded, and less vulnerable to others' attacks or manipulation so that you can better control the things you allow to influence you.

## Adopt a more productive mentality and action plan

Most people have unhelpful attitudes and practices that impede their progress toward a healthy and coherent self. This is what erodes our self-confidence and self-esteem and affects our self-efficacy. These are the sentiments and beliefs we have about our inner fundamental selves. These are counterproductive because they don't improve our quality of life in any way. Take a look at the following traits, and think about how you could display or feel them. As you do so, think about how the thought, emotion, or concept affects your self-esteem and how it affects your relationships with other people.

- You tend to personalise the opinions of others.
- When anything goes wrong at home or work, you feel everyone points the finger at you.
- You put forth a lot of effort to live up to the expectations of others, and you become down on yourself when you fall short.
- If others don't congratulate or praise you, you feel like they're pointing out your shortcomings and defects.
- You have a hard time brushing off or ignoring little irritations.
- People's unpleasant emotions, such as anger, hatred, and despair, are easy to pick up on when you're around them.
- You're always ashamed of your faults and imperfections, and you're acutely aware of them.
- You think it would be beneficial if others worked on their faults and imperfections in the same way.
- You are concerned about the quality of your connections.
- You get swept up in other people's emotions and find yourself unable to separate yourself from them.

This leads us to a discussion on how one may develop a solid sense of self-identity. Throughout the book, we'll be working on them.

**Personalisation**

Is it a common characterisation to say that you're "touchy-feely?" Have you ever been informed that you took anything personally that wasn't? Is this something that happens to you regularly? It feels like much of what people say points the finger of blame or criticism at you. Have you experienced this for most of your life or just recently? As a result of your answers, you are more likely to interpret others' words and actions as your own.

When something becomes personal to you, you begin to believe that you are the one who is being scolded, blamed, and reprimanded for not being better. Things like that hurt, particularly when they're spoken by loved ones, when you believe they're unjust, or when they're about something over which you have no authority or responsibility. In addition, when someone encourages you not to take it personally, it just exacerbates your feelings of anxiety.

**Afraid of being held responsible**

When things don't go according to plan, you may think that people blame you for their disappointment or dissatisfaction. There are various causes for this. If you're blaming yourself, here are a few plausible reasons:

- Others may openly accuse you of being the cause of the issue.
- You may still be influenced by a message you received from your parents when you were a child.
- You're responding to the current scenario the way you did when you were responsible for your parent's mental or physical well-being.
- You are an easy scapegoat to place all of the blame and accountability on.
- Others find it easy to shift responsibility, and you are willing to accept it.
- You set unreasonable goals for yourself.

Even if no one is blaming you, it's normal to feel accused when this doesn't seem to be the case. It's your fault, and you feel terrible about it. No matter how much or how little blame you place on yourself for what occurred, you still have every right to hold yourself responsible for everything that went wrong.

Taking ownership of your acts is a virtue to be nurtured, and it's a healthy habit to get into. It may seem as if you are being held responsible when you are not, when you have high expectations of yourself, or when your understanding of your influence, authority, and control is lacking.

Also, you may be wrongfully accused of anything, yet you still accept it as your duty. Others are looking for methods to avoid receiving the blame because they don't want it. In the absence of a sufficient response, the burden of proof falls on your shoulders. You may even regress and act like you did when you were blamed unjustly by a parent or sibling. Shame, guilt, and terror are possible outcomes of this chain of events.

**Disappointing others and yourself**

You may have unreasonable expectations for yourself if your self-esteem is low or if you constantly disappoint people. However, there are limitations to what you can do for others, particularly those who can care for themselves, even if they are beyond your abilities. Messages from your self-absorbed father may have influenced some of your unreasonable expectations for yourself. A few examples include:

- You are expected to please others in the same way you were required to please your parents.
- It's up to you to make sure others aren't let down.
- The needs and desires of other people are more important than your own.
- You're utterly heartbroken that you can't be better than you are.
- You tend to think that others are unhappy and that you

are to blame for not achieving their expectations, even though there is little evidence to support this.
- Anytime someone expresses dissatisfaction or disappointment with anything, it's safe to believe that person had high expectations for you.

Rather than feeling sorry for yourself all the time, save your remorse for the occasions when you fell short of your high expectations. Instead of beating yourself up or suppressing, denying, or excusing what you did, make efforts to understand your conduct better and use your dissatisfaction to motivate you to make necessary adjustments. As long as you live up to your standards, other people's acceptance is only frosting on the cake. It is not your job to make people happy all the time, nor is it your job to make sure your actions don't disappoint them. In the same way that you are not responsible for the emotions of others, you are not responsible for the feelings of others either. You may do or say something that they find unsatisfactory, but it's up to them to decide how they feel about it. You must live your life in a way that makes you proud of who you are and in line with your core principles.

**Expecting praise and appreciation**

Has your personality type been shaped by the need to get affirmation that you are acting by the expectations of your peers and so achieving their approval, or that they like you? What if you don't get these? Was there a sense that you were not good enough or that your efforts were not recognised? Acknowledging your skill, effort, and the like is always welcomed, but persistent demand for such acknowledgement may suggest a need for reassurance. A lack of praise and appreciation may be particularly damaging if you believe that another person is criticising you. Irrational thoughts and beliefs may easily hurt you since you utilise an absence (no positive feedback) to infer a negative (they intend to signal that you are defective and imperfect). For those who are self-conscious about their shortcomings, you may cling to others' praise and flattery to make up for their criticism. If you don't get favourable feedback, your wounds become worse.

It's possible that you're more concerned with getting approval from others than you are with getting approval from yourself. The energy that might be better spent on building your self-acceptance rather than trying to cover up your flaws is wasted in trying to cover up what you perceive are flaws.

## Constantly paying attention to tiny discomfort and displeasure

An inability to tolerate little irritations and annoyances is one trait that may keep you from letting go of unpleasant or painful sentiments. Staying aware of your unpleasant feelings, such as irritation, may help you think about your feelings, appraise the validity of the feelings as a danger to yourself, and recognise that you don't have to hold on to the feelings if you don't want to. If you don't let go of the bad feelings, they will only grow and worsen.

Anger and irritation may be connected to what you believe the triggering behaviours are saying about you. When you see a danger to yourself, you become agitated or annoyed. The majority of obnoxious behaviours aren't dangerous. Thus they may be disregarded. It's also bad for your health, well-being, and relationships to hang on to these annoyances.

## Observing others' emotions

Do you become agitated or irritated when you're around someone who's down, depressed, or generally in a bad mood? Do you get stiff, snarky, or abrupt in your reactions when you're around someone hostile or angry? Whenever you're dealing with too-sensitive folks, do you want to get away from them quickly? Examples of how you might experience eavesdropping on other people's thoughts and feelings are below.

By absorbing other people's suffering, resentment, anger, and other negative emotions, you may be aggravating your problems. You are more likely to get wounded or re-hurt if you allow yourself to be caught up in these sentiments, which you carry about and resonate with. It's difficult or impossible for you to detach your sentiments from someone else's and let them go, so you're stuck in the mud.

As you build your psychological boundaries, you'll be better able to resist picking up on the emotions of others. As long as you can still empathise with them, your sentiments won't become part of your own. Allowing them to express their thoughts without succumbing to any of the following is also possible:

- Being able to connect with their emotions by taking their feelings into yourself and identifying with them.
- Clinging to negative emotions and refusing to let them go.
- Feeling responsible for the emotions of another person.
- Make an effort to alleviate the other person's discomfort to make yourself feel better in the process.
- Being annoyed with yourself. Aside from occasional self-criticism, you may be acting on the sentiments of others, which is why you need to attempt to eradicate it.

It takes time and effort to establish healthy boundaries, so it's a good idea to get the help of a professional therapist to help you get there.

**Imperfections and flaws**

People all have their shortcomings, but these perceived flaws may be a major cause of guilt, humiliation, and even physical discomfort for a self-absorbed child. Irrational or not, the perceived defects and shortcomings might be true or not. When someone has a strong need to be flawless in everything they do, doing anything that is less-than-perfect may lead to feelings of guilt and self-doubt, which can be detrimental to one's well-being. Even if a person is aware that perfection is an ideal and that most mistakes aren't embarrassing, this dynamic is still in play. This is an illustration of how logic and emotions may conflict.

Being honest about your shortcomings may elicit strong feelings that cut to the heart of your basic being. After all, you want to be proud of who you are, and your basic self is what distinguishes you as a person. Everyone wants this. Some individuals never begin the lifetime process of accepting that they have faults and shortcomings. They may claim to be self-accepting, but the truth is that they reject, suppress, conceal, and disguise their genuine selves because they perceive their imperfections as undesirable. Even though you don't want to admit it to yourself, you're acutely aware of these things making you uncomfortable. Nobody can help but perceive your flaws, but you also don't seem to be able to do anything about them. You're also feeling a little down about it.

If you identify with this description, it's likely that you have trouble forgiving people and have a hard time forgiving yourself for any lapses, errors, failures, etc. I wonder why people don't strive harder to overcome their faults and shortcomings when you are so demanding. What baffles you is how people can be so tolerant of being less than ideal.

As you build yourself, you'll need to become more self-aware and embrace your imperfections. In other words, you have a new outlook on life and a new way of seeing yourself. That doesn't imply you stop striving to improve yourself. Even though you are aware of your shortcomings and imperfections, you can concentrate on your strengths and positive attributes.

**Reliance on others to share your ideals**

Some of your activities and attitudes may make you feel good about yourself, even if you're aware of your shortcomings. In other words, you may desire that others have some of your traits since it would justify your existence and make you feel more secure and self-assured.

You may privately believe that your method of doing things is the best way to go and that the world would be a better place if more people were like you. If you're a good role model, you may be able to recognise how others may improve and lessen their burdens, and you may be correct about what they should do to better themselves. You have a lot to be proud of when it comes to your character traits.

However, when others don't desire these behaviours and attitudes, openly reject your efforts to urge them to change, or don't find these traits as admirable as you do, your beliefs about others becoming more like you might expose you to hurt. Choosing to think, feel, and act differently might make you feel that others are diminishing or rejecting you. Being rejected and not understanding why others don't want to be more like you is a sad experience. From guilt and resentment against the individual who refuses to realise that your way of being is superior to theirs to anger and resentment toward yourself for being undervalued. The way you respond to a person directly impacts how you perceive and interact with them.

It would be beneficial to acknowledge and accept that you can't force people to change, that there are admirable alternative attitudes and ways of behaving, that others may find their way to more constructive behaviours, and that not being like you doesn't necessarily imply that others are wrong or terrible or ashamed. When you can accept and respect individuals for who they are, you will feel less hurt even if they are different from you. Even though it's a big change for you, you don't have to sacrifice any of your excellent characteristics to lessen or remove your hurt.

## 5

## Self-strengthening tools

YOUR KNOWLEDGE of your self-absorbed habits and attitudes is usually poor or nonexistent. You do not perceive what you are saying, doing, believing, or thinking that indicates self-absorption. Even though these habits and attitudes negatively influence you and your family, you may not be aware of the full extent of the harm they cause. You have undoubtedly attempted to bring them to the parent's notice, but the parent is ignorant of them and will discount or refute your characterisation of their actions and attitudes. It may be difficult to grasp the reality of this deficiency of perception, but it does exist. The parent just cannot see what you and others can see so plainly. Everyone, including you, has the same blindness. You're just like your parent when it comes to your self-obsessed actions and attitudes.

### Emerge from feeling broken

The first step in reducing or eliminating self-absorbed behaviours and attitudes is to accept a premise and show certain self-absorbed behaviours and attitudes. The second stage is to state to yourself that you want to become more aware of them to lessen or eliminate them. Remember that developing a new way of thinking and doing will require time, effort, and commitment. Self-awareness and self-acceptance may help you grow and mature.

Moving forward from the first two phases, it's important to identify the changes you'd want to make and the areas you want to improve. The preceding chapters provide you with knowledge and techniques to begin, and this chapter includes some recommendations for modifying certain toxic behaviours and attitudes. Although eleven actions and attitudes are outlined, this does not imply that you have all of them. There are some minor forms of each of them that you may want to consider. As a result, you'll be able to create an action plan that's unique to you and your current situation. The following are some of the more precise criteria that represent a person's tendency toward self-indulgence:

- Arrogance, scorn, and a sense of superiority are all signs of the **entitlement** mentality.
- Actions that guarantee that you are always the focus of attention—are also known as **attention-seeking**.
- Seeking external praise, regard, and acceptance is a sign of **admiration** seeking.
- **Grandiosity** and its inverse, the impoverished self—the great and inflated self and its inverse, the deflated self.
- **Absence of compassion.** Expansions of self—a lack of identification and comprehension of the boundaries between you and others.
- **Self extensions.** Unique and special—an obsessive desire to be seen as unmatched and unrivalled.
- **Exploitations.** The practice of taking advantage of others to further one's interests.
- **Negative emotions** are the inability to feel or express profound emotions other than fear or anger.
- **A lack of empathy**—the inability to comprehend or feel empathy for another' emotions.
- **Emptiness.** In its purest form, emptiness describes what we are at our heart.
- **Envy**—the conviction that others are less deserving and

less worthy than you and that they don't deserve what you desire.

Now that you are aware of your self-absorbed habits and attitudes, you may begin to lessen or perhaps eliminate some of them.

## Entitlement

When you believe that you are entitled to preferential treatment, you demonstrate an entitlement attitude. You believe that you should be forgiven for your errors and mistakes, that you should not have to feel guilty or shame for harming others, that you should be able to do or say whatever you want to others, and they should not object. This mentality implies that you are entitled to preferential treatment and that others should share your opinion. A lack of empathy for others, a lack of knowledge that others exist and are worthy, and an unconscious belief that others are aware of and accept your specialness or superiority are all part of the package.

## Attention seeking

The following are examples of attention-seeking behaviour and attitudes:

- Talking loudly, even if you know it, would annoy other people.
- Entering and exiting the room with a bang so everyone can see and hear you.
- Dressing provocatively or in a way that accentuates one's sexiness.
- "Upstage" another individual by doing anything to divert their attention.
- Getting into a battle (verbally).
- Stopping someone in the middle of a discussion
- Using clues and teases to hint at something.

The goal of these activities is to get external confirmation that you are significant, important, different, and better than others and reaffirm that you exist and are valuable. Anxiety and fear set in as a result of self-doubt, which prompts you to take action.

**Admiration seeking**

The need for affirmation that one is better and appreciated is referred to as "admiration seeking." Compliment-seeking behaviours include bragging, boasting, and begging for praise. The following are some more examples of believing and feeling that you deserve recognition:

- Becoming more worthy than others.
- Possessing innate competence and skill.
- Having more things or more expensive ones than others.
- Having an advantage over others.
- Achieving and completing goals.
- Any additional ties you have to the area (status).

Just a few examples are given here. A person's desire to acquire the admiration of other people isn't a bad thing, but if they do it just to impress others, it isn't a good thing either. Taking pride in who you are and what you've accomplished is healthy and inspiring. On the other hand, admiration extends beyond a simple need for praise and recognition to a more aggressive demand for others' acceptance, praise, and even jealousy. Such a self-centred attitude may be curbed or even reversed.

**Grandiosity**

There are subtle indicators of grandiosity that suggest an overestimation of one's importance. They are not conscious of what is being disclosed to them, and even if this is made out to them, they are unlikely to accept that perspective even if it is pointed out to them. An overestimation of oneself, a sense of superiority, and an expansiveness that does not recognise limits or limitations are all characteristics of this attitude. I'm not only referring to the apparent indicators of grandiosity but also to the thoughts and concepts that seem sensible to the individual in question but are foolish, impractical, and illogical. The following are a few examples of this understated grandiosity:

- Immediate control of the discussion or whatever is going place.
- Taking on too many obligations, such as the inability to say no when you are already overcommitted.
- The belief that your work is superior to that of others.
- Superman/Superwoman.
- Arrogance.
- Contempt for others and a belief that they are inferior.
- Not being able to perceive the value in the thoughts or perspectives of others.
- The need to "have" or "do" everything.

Your grandiosity is probably hiding in plain sight, but you're just not paying attention.

**Absence of compassion**

Your relationships will suffer if you lack empathy, display highly toxic behaviour, and a bad attitude. Empathy is the ability to feel and understand what another person is going through. You don't simply hear the words; you feel and comprehend the underlying meaning behind the words on a far more profound level. Listening to content is vital, but the true message is in the speaker's sentiments (sender), and your capacity to empathise decides whether you can hear the underlying message behind the words. Relationships may be challenging for those who cannot empathise. This is especially true for personal relationships.

Remember that you can't empathise with everyone all of the time, so let's start there. Even the most talented and experienced physicians are unable to accomplish this. If you are emotionally vulnerable or lack psychological boundary strength, it might be risky to open yourself up to accepting other people's sentiments. As an adult with some degree of healthy self-reflection, you may be able to empathise with a wide range of individuals at various points in their lives.

**Self-extensions**

While they may be aware of the existence of other people in the world, toxic people tend to believe that others exist simply to serve them. Even if this notion is similar to that of newborns and toddlers, an adult is acting on it. As if they were the only actual people in the world, these toxic people see everything in terms of themselves, as if others were just shadows to be ordered about.

These people's lack of regard for others' boundaries may be at least in part attributed to their irrational attitudes. For them, there are no boundaries since they see everyone else as a dependent and under their control; therefore, they feel that they should be able to do or say anything they like. The following are examples of actions that demonstrate this attitude:

- Taking something from someone else without their consent.
- Refusing to speak with family members before making social or other plans
- Making decisions and having talks on behalf of those who can make their own decisions.
- Entering someone else's home or workplace without first knocking and requesting permission.
- Invading someone's personal space without their consent.
- Inquiring about personal matters such as how much something costs, when you're getting married, why you don't have children, etc.

**Special and distinctive**

We all want to be recognised as a unique individual who has something to contribute to the world. Only the selfish carry this urge to the extreme, expecting that everyone should bow to their authority and respect them above all others. As a result, these individuals believe that they are the only ones capable of reaching their level of excellence in any given field. As a result, they believe that all other people must admire and defer to them because of their uniqueness. Self-centred individuals may be unable to see the value and uniqueness of others because of their inability to respect others' rights. The following are examples of attitudes and actions that show this personality trait:

- Self-serving words and statements.
- Constantly criticising people for their mistakes and inadequacies.
- Often discussing what others should and should not be and do.
- Making unfavourable comparisons between oneself and others.
- Blaming others when obstacles arise.
- Commenting on how well the individual executes all of their work.
- Expecting to be picked, commended, and acknowledged for one's accomplishments before others.

Self-centred individuals lack empathy for others, believe they are the only ones of their kind in the world and aren't aware of the harm they are doing to others by their selfish actions and attitudes.

**Exploitation**

Exploitation is the act of taking advantage of another individual. Along with this comes the belief that others are unworthy, exist only to serve the exploiter, and are in some way inferior to the exploiter. People with a Destructive Narcissistic Pattern take advantage of everyone, but those closest to them bear the brunt of the harm, as the bond between them serves as a vehicle for the abuse to flourish. Personality elements such as care, good nature, desire to please, and need for acceptance are used by a toxic person ignoring these traits.

Other people's well-being is put at risk to accommodate a DNP sufferer's requirements. Examples of unethical behaviour include:

- Taking out a loan and not returning it.
- Expecting benefits for oneself, but not offering them back in return.
- Pushing or cajoling a person so that they will do something that is not in their best interests, but rather in the interests of the self-centred individual.
- Benefitting from dishonesty and deceitful tactics.
- Using the phrase "If you loved me" or "If you cared about me" to manipulate someone into doing something they would rather avoid.
- You can add to the list plenty of additional exploitative activities, particularly if you have a self-absorbed parent. Did your parent ever do this?
- Expect you to stop what you're doing and help them.
- Be prepared to put the needs and desires of the parent first and foremost.
- They'll point the finger at you and say that you're to blame for their unhappiness.
- Use shame or guilt to get you to do something you don't want to.
- Make fun of you for not anticipating your parents' needs and fulfilling them.
- Expect your parents to see you how they see themselves.

What if we reverse those habits and attitudes to see how we may be exploiting others? I know you don't think you're doing anything wrong, but your core inner self may be behaving in ways you aren't even aware of. Take a thorough look at all of the items on both lists, and think about how you behave and say things in your most personal family, professional, social, and other connections. Change these practices and attitudes to improve yourself.

**Negative Emotions**

Adults who have a healthy dose of narcissism are capable of feeling and expressing a broad range of emotions. On the other hand, adults are severely restricted in their ability to experience and express their emotions. For them, the range of sensations they can convey verbally is restricted to fear and fury; they have the words but not the feelings to go along with them. Except for the many manifestations of fear and anger, these folks aren't being sincere when they convey their sentiments.

**Emptiness**

The lack of anything and the presence of boundaries, such as those surrounding a hole, are common definitions for the condition of being "empty." There are no defined boundaries or defining points in the psychological condition of emptiness, making it even more difficult to characterise. Nothing exists. Some descriptions are provided below, although they do not represent the emptiness of self-absorbed individuals completely.

The self's core is empty, and any or all of the following traits are missing:

- Relationships that matter.
- The ability to communicate with the rest of the universe (inspiration or spirituality).
- Ability to experience a wide range of emotions.
- The ability to empathise with the feelings of others.
- The ability to feel empathy and compassion for others.
- A sense of awe and astonishment at the world's natural splendour.
- Self is a unique and distinct entity with intrinsic value.
- Capacity to love and appreciate oneself and others.
- Self-sacrifice for the sake of others.

No other state is known to the empty individual. Thus he or she thinks everyone else is as empty in their heart. There is nothing outside of the individual that can fill the void. The needs to come from inside, and it's possible that person isn't even aware of the hole they're trying to fill.

Many individuals who don't hold a DNP may be missing something at the heart of their being. In any case, they are aware of the issues and are taking action to address them. People with DNP have a hollow centre; they may feel a void but cannot pinpoint what it is. They want what others have but can't identify what they want, so they get it themselves. Reflection and self-growth are often replaced by activity in the lives of certain individuals. In addition, the following may be used instead:

- Abuse of drugs or alcohol.
- Blind commitment to a "calling," such as a cult, a religion, or a charismatic individual.
- Gambling.
- Overeating and undereating.
- Overspending when shopping.
- Excessive involvement in the community, social, and other causes.
- It's impossible to fill the hole, yet they keep looking for a way to fill it.
- Is there anything that can be done to avoid and overcome emptiness?
- Relationships that are long-lasting, meaningful, and gratifying.
- Life's purpose and meaning.
- A wonderful and uplifting part of life.
- Reaching out to people and making a positive impact on their life.
- Increasing one's capacity for creativity, empathy, and sage judgment.

**Envy**

Envy may be defined as a desire for another person's possessions and the belief that one is more worthy than the other. While jealousy has all of these components, it is the most destructive second.

Desire may be both a motivator and a difficulty in the quest to get one's desired goal. For example, if you want to get a promotion, you may put in the effort to get it. Or, if you'd want to be wealthy, you might look for methods to do it. If you're determined to succeed, you can build relationships, define and attain success, acquire skills, and set objectives. In most circumstances, they are all achievable goals.

Wanting something may quickly turn into envy if it is accompanied by bitterness over the fact that someone else has it, especially if you believe that they are less worthy or undeserving than you are. Instead of striving to achieve your goals, time and energy are squandered on resentment at the other person, worrying about how you were treated unjustly, or attempting to persuade others to see the other person in the same light you do, which is deserved and unworthy—these sentiments of injustice and wrath damage your self-worth and soul.

Although you may be right and more deserving, it won't help you achieve your objective even if we assume you are correct. And you're just hurting yourself by harbouring bitterness and believing you've been treated unfairly. Other people are not harming you by giving you what you desire, whether they deserve it. You're allowing the bad effects to keep you from attaining your goals, detrimental to your progress.

## Goals for a less self-absorbed person

If you want to replace your self-centred habits with more self-aware ones, it may help to create some objectives for yourself and put them into words. There's a fine line between being self-reflective and being able to put the well-being of others ahead of your own when it's in the best interest of everyone. Your basic self is not sacrificed for others, but you give of yourself when their need is greater than your own, and you actively choose to do so. Maintaining your core inner self and being able to connect with others is an important part of your well-being.

There's an underlying idea that everything revolves around you. You've got to shake that one off. Self-obsessed behaviour is reduced while self-awareness and empathy for others are increased.

Listed below are a few potential aims and ideas for behavioural adjustments. Behaving differently tends to change your outlook. Make a mental note of what you'll do and say after you've achieved your aim of lessening or eliminating a self-centred outlook or habit. Think about it: You may not even be aware of your self-absorbed conduct or attitude. That's why you must take all of the advice into account.

**Purpose and meaning beyond self-absorption**

You'll desire greater meaning and purpose in your life after reducing your self-absorption and developing healthy adult narcissism. Meaning and purpose enrich our lives, link us to the world around us, and allow us to appreciate our time here on Earth. As a result, loneliness and alienation may be reduced or eliminated; overcoming despair, hopelessness, and helplessness; embracing oneself; acquiring more realistic expectations of yourself and others; recognising the limitations of your responsibility, and being more grounded.

What parts of your life may have significance and purpose for you? Are you aware of these aspects? Are there parts of your life that make you happy? Are there parts of your life that are dissatisfied or displeased? How can you take action to improve these areas? You might also attempt to better understand what and how you want your life to be. Now it's time to talk about the advantages of starting this project.

**Isolation and disconnection**

Emotionally and psychologically, this is characterised by a sense of isolation and loneliness and an inability to perceive how you might make good changes in your life. Even though it sounds like depression, this description lacks the clinical and physical characteristics of the illness. All of us face this question at some point in our lives. In situations when your sense of purpose and meaning in life isn't quite what you'd want it to be, this feeling might creep in and make an appearance.

Having a sense of loneliness or alienation is like being lost in space, unable to locate oneself in any of the following ways:

- Personal relationships that provide you joy.
- Pleasure, enjoyment, and amusement.
- A feeling of being sought for and appreciated.
- Seeing that your efforts are valued and beneficial.
- Having a strong sense of self-confidence and competence in many areas of your life.

In the absence of these anchors, you may begin to feel alone and unconnected. These sentiments might grow into feelings of isolation and hostility if they are not addressed.

**A sense of despair, helplessness, and a lack of belief**

Discouragement and sadness are two milder forms of despair. Among the lesser forms of helplessness are ineffectiveness and impotence. There are many minor forms of despair, such as a sense that things are dismal or bleak. This is because you may not be aware that you are experiencing some weaker forms of these sensations, even if they are less intense. These things might also lead to your life having little or no meaning and purpose.

You can't control what you believe is within your control, which causes despair, helplessness, and hopelessness in your life. It's possible that you're feeling discouraged, sad, or hopeless because of how you see things. There is a possibility that the talk about extensions of self may be influencing your thoughts of how much influence you have over others; that is, where you believe they are or should be. Ineffectiveness might set in if they don't do what you want them to. You refuse to acknowledge that you did not influence them and don't have control over them now or in the future. To let go of the delusion that others should do what you want them to, you must first recognise and accept that you are different from others on a conscious and unconscious level and then focus on developing your narcissism.

Many things in life are out of your hands, such as the state of the economy, and the words and deeds of others. Wars, for example, are just too huge and complicated to be managed by a single person. Realise that certain things are under your control and others are beyond your control. Instead of despair, helplessness, and hopelessness, this shift will save you from falling into those negative emotions. You must, however, let go of any fantasies that you have regarding the following:

- Making someone fall in love with you.
- Transforming another person.
- Expecting the world to always be fair and just.
- Want to be given special consideration.
- Influencing the words and actions of others.

Think of your core self as being the only one in the world.

**Changes that lead to self-acceptance and growth**

As you read this book and worked through the activities, you may have discovered elements of your core inner self that you were previously unaware of. You may also have discovered certain habits and attitudes that may be modified, and you may feel ashamed or disgraced about some aspects of your core inner self. Be at ease. We've all been there and can always benefit from further growing and developing, particularly to foster a strong sense of self-importance in the later years.

One of the most difficult things you'll have to learn is to accept who you are on the inside, with all of your flaws and shortcomings. Keep in mind that you are not denying or exaggerating any part of your true inner self. Never, ever, ever give up since it will just slow down your development. The more you think and concentrate on what's going well in your life, the better off you'll be.

You may improve your self-esteem by using positive self-talk. You're not ignoring or dismissing your perceived shortcomings;

rather, you're working with them to create constructive change. It's crucial to be patient with yourself and keep trying despite setbacks and failures.

**The need for more accurate expectations**

You may have to lower your standards, both for yourself and for others. Expecting perfection from yourself and others is a good illustration of this. Unrealistic expectations may lead to the following outcomes:

- When anything goes wrong or isn't flawless, don't blame anybody except yourself.
- When your expectations aren't realised, even if they aren't stated, and you expect the other person to know what's on your mind, you may act and speak in ways that harm a relationship.
- Embarrassing yourself and blaming others, even those who are close to you.
- Constantly worrying that you're going to screw up.
- Your health, self-esteem, and relationships are all affected by these factors.

A common kind of expectation is a demand that people do things your way, even though it would be completely fair to let them do it their way, such as filling the dishwasher in the opposite direction that you would do it. On the other hand, your assumption that others would automatically understand what you want or need and fulfil it is irrational. When this occurs to you, it might be a pleasant surprise, but it can be a less pleasant surprise when it becomes an expectation for you.

On the other side, having high expectations for oneself might be a good thing. High expectations, not ridiculous ones, are what I meant. There is nothing wrong, for example, with striving for perfection. Negative behaviour occurs when you expect it from others and yourself and when you refuse to accept anything less than perfection. You'll never be happy with yourself or others since you'll never achieve perfection. As a result of others' lack of desire for perfection, your relationships suffer. This second posture or mentality does not result in guilt, shame, persistent worry, or discontent, and these are compelling reasons to strive for more realistic expectations of yourself and others.

**Putting a stop to your self-destructive behaviour**

If you haven't completely come to know your core inner self as different from others, you haven't grasped that there are boundaries to your accountability. In addition, you may be blaming yourself, feeling humiliated, thinking you're ineffective and attempting to exert control over people and circumstances that you can't manage. This is all unnecessary. Boundary strength is a factor in these difficulties. Boundaries that can withstand pressure are ideal, but you may also have spongy, hard, or soft ones.

The following examples may help you better understand your responsibilities:

- When someone says that you made them feel a certain way, do you apologise or say that wasn't what you meant to do?
- When someone forces you to do something you don't want to, do you have the confidence to stand your ground?
- To please someone else or avoid disappointing someone else, have you broken any of your standards, ethics, or values?
- Does it make you feel awful (shamed or guilty) when you cause discomfort in another person?
- Do you put yourself in harm's way to safeguard the happiness of others?
- Do you suppress your emotions or desires so that others would not be bothered by your sentiments or desires?

If any or all of these apply to you, you're taking on too much responsibility. You're not aware of the boundaries of your obligation to care for others; neither are you willing to acknowledge or admit that there are any. It's not as if you don't have a duty to treat people with respect, tact, and sensitivity. In doing so, you'll be able to build stronger connections. However, suppose you engage in any of the above behaviours, emotions, or thoughts. In that case, it's a sign that you've gone too far in your attempts to connect and that you're neglecting your own needs and failing to acknowledge that you are not the other person. People choose to feel a certain way for several reasons outside their control, and you have no power over how they choose to feel. Even if anything in their surroundings causes them to feel this way, it's not your obligation to do something about it.

**Getting grounded and centred**

Self-absorption has been addressed in this chapter, and the advantages of self-improvement have been described in detail. These advantages and some others discussed in the next chapter may help you become more focused and grounded. You won't go off track and do activities that don't contribute to your overall happiness and well-being or a meaningful and purposeful existence.

You can behave in line with your ideals and resist the influence of others.

As a result of adversity, you don't break apart, melt down, or isolate yourself.

Amidst difficult and distressing situations, you may keep your sense of your core self.

You can accept being alone without feeling lonely.

You choose connections that benefit both parties.

Work to strengthen yourself and improve the aspects of yourself you want to change.

Your ability to fight despair, hopelessness, and helplessness means that you can go forward.

To deal with the ups and downs of life with some peace of mind, it helps to have a firm sense of self-centredness and a sense of stability. Even though you may not achieve your goals, you may rest comfortably that you've done your best and that what you have accomplished and who you are are good enough. You can accept your shortcomings without feeling shameful and must be concealed at all costs, and you can let others manage and control their own life, ideas, and emotions. Becoming more grounded and focused may have a wide range of benefits for you and your life.

You'll be less likely to get narcissistically wounded if you can keep your head straight and your feet firmly on the ground. It is impossible to avoid getting hurt, but you may lessen your susceptibility by strengthening your sense of self, fostering a healthy sense of adult narcissism, and setting clear and protective boundaries. You'll also find it simpler to perform the following things:

- Take a deep breath and let go of any lingering feelings of bitterness or anger.
- Stop associating with and adopting the projections of others (projective identification).
- Accept and respect others' differences.
- Build and sustain significant and rewarding friendships and connections.
- Have a purposeful and meaningful existence.

In the next chapter, you'll find ideas and tactics to help you grow and develop as a person so that you may let go of even more painful situations and move forward in healing. Other painful memories and resentments from your past may be mostly forgotten, but you may still have a few lingering resentments. In addition, you may have been able to lessen or remove your sentiments about these incidents and any lingering bad consequences. You've made a lot of progress, and you should congratulate yourself. You still have a long way to go, but you're making progress!

# 6

# Define the person you want to be

It's CONCEIVABLE, but not likely, that you'll experience an immediate shift because you're a complicated individual with many sides of your basic inner self that you're unaware of. Attempting to implement a slew of large changes at once is usually a bad idea since it is unlikely that any of them will succeed. It is suggested that you begin by making gradual adjustments over time. The more you learn about yourself, the more you'll be able to change and grow. This is especially true if you're working to overcome narcissistic wounds and other aspects of self-absorption.

In the next sections, you'll learn to strengthen your basic inner self and make it less susceptible to being injured by your toxic parent. You've already gotten some advice from the book, but here is some more. Some of it may not be appropriate or possible for you, in which case it would be unreasonable for you to use the advice. If any of these ideas resonate with you at this point, go with them. After you've tried them, you may check whether the ones you set aside are still useful.

## Changing perceptions: Developing a new way of thinking

In this book's previous chapters, you have already begun to build awareness by completing some or all exercises. To some extent, you are more aware of what you are going through right now, how your upbringing and past experiences have shaped who you are, what drives your thoughts and feelings, how strong and adaptable your psychological boundaries are, and even to what extent your narcissism is still under-developed. In your search for meaning and purpose, you've discovered beneficial traits that may keep you grounded and focused in your life. What you've accomplished here is enormous. To become the person you picture, there are further steps you may take.

Fully functioning persons who are aware of the fact that life is a fleeting experience, as well as those who are aware of the following:

- They appreciate the current moment.
- They are interconnected with the rest of creation.
- Wonder and beauty may be seen in everything around them.
- They need to listen to what their bodies are telling them.
- When listening to others, they can be emotionally present to the fullest extent.
- There is no conflict between their thoughts and actions.
- They make their norms, ideals, and values known and freely chosen.
- They're able to accept the facts.
- They can recognise and access their emotions.

Appreciating the present moment allows you to be more present in your life. As significant as the past is, you must also realise that it has no bearing on how you operate or how happy you are in the current moment. There is no way to tell how much of the future will be experienced; therefore, speculating about it is pointless and may take away from the present moment's richness.

When you're a part of the world, you can love and be loved and feel less lonely and alone. You are not completely at the mercy of elements beyond your control, whether physical, mental, or spiritual. The enormity of the universe is intimidating but not dangerous. There's a lot to learn.

Contemplate: Are you a meditator or a prayer? Describe the process you use to establish a connection with something greater than yourself. Do you have a ritual that helps you to re-energise your spirit?

The ability to appreciate wonder and beauty in the world focuses on the potential in your surroundings rather than the negative. Feeling helpless and impotent to cope with misfortune is an easy way to fall into hopelessness and despair when caught up in the injustice of other people and circumstances. Many of these negatives may be found easily. The positives, such as astonishment and beauty, are more difficult to concentrate on. Every day, make an effort to observe the wonder and beauty surrounding you.

Listening to your body's cues might help you remain grounded and better comprehend your thoughts and feelings. Despite your best efforts to alter some aspects of your inherent inner self, you can recognise the responses you are experiencing and understand why you are behaving the way you are.

You may hear the overt and hidden meanings in the conversation, connect with the other person in a meaningful manner, and better comprehend what they're going through if you're emotionally present while listening to people. Do not interrupt the other person by asking questions instead of reacting empathically. You are not distracted by thoughts of other topics. Do not change the subject or do anything other than put your thoughts and emotions into listening.

The mind and body react in sync and are always communicating with one another. The mind and body are not engaged in different activities simultaneously. The symmetry of this arrangement enhances mindfulness and attentiveness.

Choose your standards, ideals, and values instead of following what you've been "taught" or what others value and have pushed on you. As a result, it's not a good idea to throw out the old rules and concepts. These may be preserved, but you decided to keep them open and straightforward rather than being forced upon you. Your existing position and personality are considered while creating new options for you.

Try to embrace reality without romanticising it and ignoring the good or bad sides of the situation. Make an effort to understand how your vision may be skewed as well. Reality's more sombre features aren't downplayed, but they're also not overemphasised to the point where it's pointless to go on. Acceptance of reality is a mature attitude that may catalyse taking action to improve reality.

Feel your emotions and identify what they are. One of the most important things you've done so far is getting a deeper knowledge of both yourself and the people around you. These aren't little or superficial feelings. They're a lot of feelings. This is a vital source of knowledge for you since you are not afraid to know what you are experiencing at all times. Even if your sentiments aren't always logical and sensible, it doesn't mean they aren't still useful and instructive.

**Change your perspective: Lessen your self-absorption**

Self-absorbed behaviour and attitudes are relatively simple to see in others but not easy to spot in yourself. You should acknowledge that you undoubtedly have some of them, but you should also attempt to lessen the self-centred actions and attitudes you may be aware of and those you are unaware of.

Don't be so pretentious. Reduce the number of items on your to-do list if you feel inundated or overwhelmed. Allow yourself to delegate some of those chores, and understand that certain jobs don't need to be done perfectly—good enough will suffice.

Reduce your need for attention. For example, do not hide your sicknesses or discomforts from others, but downplay them unless they can help you. Get into the practice of just discussing your symptoms when you need help.

Reduce the inability to empathise. Even though a person's worry is unimportant to you, you should try to address their emotions. Even though you may not have an answer for the problem, acknowledging and responding to the person's sentiments is a positive and useful response.

Cut down on your self-esteem. Use your positive self-statements whenever you sense self-doubt, self-blame, or thoughts of inadequacy to remind yourself of your strengths and skills. You may even tell yourself that you've made progress in the areas you're working to improve yourself.

Fill up the gap. Meaning and purpose may be found in various ways, including meaningful relationships, productive work, inspiration, and appreciation of the natural environment. Doing good actions and being part of a good cause are two ways to improve one's quality of life. Reach out and connect with people genuinely and appreciatively.

Reduce or eradicate the feeling of enviously. Being jealous of another' accomplishments, prosperity, or ability is relatively simple and frequent. Instead, you may spend your time and energy strengthening your abilities and learning new things. When I'm jealous, I think about what I'd have to give up to have what I'm envious of.

You may lessen your selfish tendencies and attitudes while simultaneously increasing your capacity for self-reflection by cultivating a healthy level of adult narcissism. Both are essential to avoid or minimise the damage caused by narcissistic wounds. It may seem contradictory to be both self-absorbed and self-reflective at the same time, yet a unified, focused, and grounded self needs a balance between the two.

**Self-reflection as a perceptual shift**

You can use self-reflection to examine your actions, feelings, and thoughts to see if you're exhibiting self-absorbed behaviours and attitudes, whether your boundaries are strong and resilient, if you're failing to consider the needs of the other person, or if you're in danger of becoming entangled or overwhelmed. Even if you're completely self-obsessed, you're still focused on yourself, but differently.

Building awareness of what you and others are thinking and feeling in the present moment is the first step in increasing your self-reflection and decreasing your self-absorption. The following are some ideas for increasing your level of awareness:

- Make an effort to name, classify, and identify your feelings regularly.
- Try to get a sense of what others are going through.
- Be on the lookout for projection or transference in your emotions.
- Feelings may be deceiving, so be aware of this.
- When communicating with others, keep in mind your limitations in terms of personal accountability.

Feelings are a natural part of life; they are not something that should be stifled by anybody else. You own them, and you should treat them as such. However, suppose you add in your personality. In that case, your family-of-origin experiences, other prior events, the level of your self-absorption, and your emotional vulnerability, you might be misled by your sentiments. A lot goes into determining how you feel, and these are some of the primary factors. Even if you aren't aware of it, you automatically respond to these fundamental aspects regardless of whether you are consciously aware. Some unpleasant sentiments may become less severe; you'll be able to respond more constructively externally; your inclination to personalise what others say and do will be reduced; and you'll be able to focus on others instead of focusing on yourself all the time.

# 7

## Create a new and better you

LET's take a look at the person you want to be so that you may assess whether or not the ideal self that you want to become is practical and attainable or whether you have unrealistic and unattainable objectives. Achieving goals with a high likelihood of success can help you feel better about yourself and boost your positive feelings about your abilities. You may also determine where you need to change and where you've made adjustments that have gotten you closer to your goal by comparing your existing self to your ideal self.

Let's take a quick look back at everything we've covered before we continue. There are many ways to strengthen your essential inner self, including ways to build meaning and purpose for your life that reflect your values and principles; ways to reduce or eliminate feelings of isolation and alienation; ways to reduce or eliminate self-absorbed behaviours and attitudes that may be negatively impacting your relationships; and ways to become more centred so that your choices and decisions are not undue.

By enhancing awareness in the present, explaining how self-reflection is important, utilising your strengths, and discovering and using your psychological limits, Chapter 6 provided further information on building your core inner self. What you can do to live more completely was the main focus.

How to deal with your toxic parent as an adult and how to build and sustain meaningful connections while dealing with your vital inner self are all topics covered in this chapter. Here, you'll learn about the lasting effects of your early life experiences, the importance of responding to others with empathy and reflection when dealing with a selfish parent, and practical steps you can take to improve your emotional well-being while also strengthening your interpersonal connections.

## The influence of early life events on your personality

As you get older, your fundamental inner self is shaped by the interactions of the care and nurture you got from your family of origin, your prior encounters with individuals other than your family of origin, and personality qualities that are inherently yours. There is no one-size-fits-all personality type, and even persons from the same social and cultural contexts might exhibit slight differences.

Researchers and theorists have accumulated a wealth of information on how children's psychological well-being is shaped. They consistently point to the importance of receiving high-quality early care and nurturing. Early here refers to birth through the first years of a child's development. Prenatal impacts have been studied. However, they have not been linked to the formation of the self's psychological self and are more focused on physical factors that may play a role in developing the self's psychology. We shall not investigate this knowledge since it has no connection to the growth of the mind.

"How did you become the person you are today?" is the most fundamental question. Using the knowledge provided here, you may look at your psychological growth and discover why you may be feeling narcissistically wounded, get a fresh point of view, and learn how to protect yourself from further trauma. Understanding some of the various effects and experiences you may have had in the past may be beneficial.

Let's start with some early signals about how your parents and siblings saw you.

You may have been influenced by others' perceptions of your

physical appearance, intellect, skills, or other attributes in the past, rather than your current reality or experience.

If you don't take the time to think about these early signals, you may not even be aware of their presence until you do so. When you were a child, you automatically assimilated them into your identity and associated with them without realising it. To what degree you become narcissistically wounded in encounters with your self-absorbed parent may depend on the strength of these early unconscious signals that continue to influence your self-perception. Using reflective listening and reacting, you may better control your interactions with the parent in the next part.

## Responding to your self-absorbed parent with compassion and introspection

In this part, we'll talk about dealing with your self-absorbed parent. Other encounters and relationships may also benefit from it. If you can master the art of contemplative listening and response, you'll be more productive. Even if you can't empathise with the selfish parent, it doesn't mean you shouldn't pay attention to the emotions displayed in their conversations and interactions. Identifying the difference between empathy and a more helpful response to your parent's sentiments is the first step. The parent will feel heard and understood if you do this, and you won't have to agree with or buy into the parent's message or sentiments to do this.

Do you mix up empathy with sympathy? Even if your parent is self-absorbed, there is no need to react or empathise with them to expose yourself to the possibility of picking up on their sentiments or projections and acting on them. You don't have to either allow yourself to be entirely consumed by another person's emotions or block them off altogether. Being able to employ reflective responses with your self-absorbed parent and others might benefit you. Unlike empathetic response, reflective responding does not need you to experience what another person feels. Four stages are involved in reflective responding:

1. Determine the other person's emotion (whether that person expresses that feeling directly or indirectly).
2. Put yourself in the other person's shoes and express how you feel without repeating precisely what they said or what you believe they meant. Do not introduce a new idea or pose a new question to the contemplation. "You seem annoyed," is one example.
3. Before contributing or asking a question, get confirmation or denial of your identification of the experience. If the other person finds an error in your argument or doesn't agree with your choice of words, they will correct you. It is possible that their answer to you portraying their wrath would be to respond, "I'm just irritated," instead of "Angry." Wait for the other to expound or clarify before you continue speaking. Accept the person's correction of your feelings.
4. You have the opportunity to offer a comment or ask a question at this moment. Avoid bringing up counter-arguments or expressing your own opinion before the arrogant parent. Recognition of another person's emotions is a primary objective.

A helpful skill to develop when you begin to express yourself reflectively is recognising the emotion portrayed by someone else, even if they don't say it out loud. As an example, how may the speaker feel about these statements?

**"What a great person you are!"**
**"It's making me nervous."**
**"I'd say it's a wonderful day."**
**"This does not sit well with me."**
**"What's the point?"**

You may be able to figure out how the speaker feels if you know them well. Although it is possible to be mistaken even if one believes he or she knows the individual, it is more probable that one is correct. People assume they're speaking clearly and honestly, yet their sentiments are hidden and indirect. For any remark, there might be a range of emotions. The sensations are thus hard to pin down.

## Gaining strength through creative activities

Creativity comes in various shapes and sizes. A good place to start is by being more open and aware of your creative potential and your creative efforts and the wide variety of options that exist for them. When it comes to being creative, you don't have to confine yourself to the idea that you must be an artist. As a result, you may believe that only certain individuals are creative, that you can only be creative in one of two ways, or that you must have an inborn skill or capability. People who have been recognised for their abilities and ingenuity appear to suit the last definition. However, this definition and description of healthy adult narcissism may be applied to anybody. Because they can be learned, they are not reliant on a person's natural ability.

In this context, the term "creativity" refers to the ability to come up with new ideas and approaches to old problems and the willingness to try something new, learn something new, and put that knowledge to good use. It also refers to the ability to develop new ways of doing things and find solutions to old problems. Many people have heard the expression "thinking outside the box." This is true. To think outside the box, you must be open to new ideas and open to doing things that have never been attempted before. The first stage is to be open to receiving new information, opinions, and perspectives.

Engaging in creative activities may accomplish the following:

- Boost your sense of well-being and happiness in all areas of your life.
- You'll find it simpler to block off distractions, fears, and other issues for a while.
- Support in the process of mending the innermost wounds of one's being.
- Learn about areas of yourself that you've been ignoring or haven't even known to exist.

Nonetheless, not all of the advantages pertain only to you. As a result of thinking creatively, you can do things such as create new meals for your family, beautify your home or yard, save money by fixing things that don't work, and inspire and support others. You can also demonstrate problem-solving that teaches others how to solve their problems better, and you can encourage and support other people in their endeavours. Enthusiasm and a sense of wonder may be contagious when you model them.

Teaching through example how to be open and receptive to problems is what you're doing right now.

Having a zest and enthusiasm in your life results from being creative rather than confined to your thoughts and feelings. It's a win-win situation for you and your imagination.

Your task will be to create your unique technique for unleashing your creative juices. Don't give up; it will take a lot of experimenting until you discover what works for you. You'll find it if you keep trying. The following are a few options for getting started:

- Take a look back at what you enjoyed doing as a child and see whether it may be transformed into something creative now.
- Take a course in something you're interested in.
- Buy a kit from a craft shop and finish it yourself.
- Try out some new dishes from your cookbook, a magazine, or the internet.
- Sketch the environment you find yourself in.
- You don't have to limit yourself to poetry or prose; you may write about whatever you choose.
- Find a new purpose for something you're about to toss away and save money.

It's up to you to define what constitutes "creativity" for you. Don't hesitate; just go forward and execute your plan.

## Having a sense of purpose

There is evidence that spirituality or inspiration may have a physical, emotional, and psychological impact. It includes religion, but it goes further than that. If you're spiritual, you don't need to be religious. The word "inspirational" has been chosen since many people will reject "spirituality" because they believe you're referring to religion. During this time, you'll be able to transcend your existence and connect with the universe. When you experience a sense of profound connection to the universe as a part of your existence, you might feel less alone and alienated, even when you are completely alone. This is what it means to be inspirational.

You may strengthen your ties to yourself, others, and the cosmos by being inspired or searching for inspiration. It may also alleviate emotions of loneliness and alienation and a general sense of disorientation. Inspiration may help you regain your sense of centre and establish a more solid foundation for your life.

What's the point of cultivating a creative mindset? How may this help in letting go of resentments, grudges, and the like? Does inspiration have any effect on the occurrence of narcissistic trauma? As with so many other parts of your life, inspiration operates in various indirect ways. Improved self-acceptance means that you'll be happier and less likely to dwell on the negative aspects of yourself and others. You learn to concentrate on the essential aspects of your life rather than becoming bogged down in the minutiae of daily living.

We spoke about how narcissistic injury includes a sense of powerlessness and despair earlier in the book. One thing that prevents the wounds from healing is the feelings of guilt and shame that they might elicit. The negative consequences on oneself may sometimes be mitigated only to a certain extent by external support and acceptance, optimistic self-talk, or even success itself. Many examples of individuals who have achieved great success but continue to engage in self-destructive behaviour or write about how they don't feel they are talented enough. Such cases demonstrate how narcissistic injury may be both debilitating and long-lasting.

There is a good chance that you've done some work in healing your wounds and growing and strengthening your fundamental inner self to avoid, eliminate, or minimise this hurting. Work hard, and your skills improve. An additional beneficial step that will pay off with excellent results is to inspire.

There are various methods available for connecting with and enhancing your inspiring life.

Your career, or even your contribution to others, may provide you with opportunities to tap into this reservoir. No matter how you get there, you will discover that it uplifts and strengthens your spirit, aids in meaning and purpose, inoculates and sustains your resistance, and raises your awareness and appreciation of life. It is a great way to live your life to its fullest.

The following are some more techniques to come in touch with your inspiration. Select the ones that work best for you, try a few that you've never tried before, and see what happens. None of them will work right now, but they all have a chance to work in the long run.

- Meditation.
- Religion and worship.
- Efforts at art.
- Reading uplifting content.
- Creating a written record of your feelings.
- Ceremonies of centring and anchoring.
- Cultivating and enhancing relationships.

### Fairness, integrity, and collaboration

A healthy relationship is built on mutual respect's individuality, worth, and value. You want to be valued, you want to feel important, and you want to be reciprocated by showing the other person how much you value their presence in your life by doing the same for them. It's important to remember that acceptance, like respect, focuses on others rather than on what you want them to be or what you hope they will become. Just because you've accepted yourself doesn't mean you can't or shouldn't make changes. For example, if the other person values neatness and tends to be messy, you may wish to strive to be neater if the demand for neatness is not too high.

## Become empathic in your relationships

Empathy is a fantastic feeling in which the individual feels completely understood. It's a once-in-a-lifetime opportunity. As some people believe, empathy is not a condition of being overwhelmed or engulfed in another person's emotions. These are cognitive reactions in the case of sympathy, and a lack of boundary strength in the other two is the cause of these behavioural responses. Being empathetic means tuning into and feeling what the other person is feeling without losing sight of who you are as a unique individual. When you are not overwhelmed or involved, you are not left with leftover sensations that you are unwilling to let go of.

The reciprocal nature of empathy is also vital in relationships, so it is so important to cultivate empathy. You must be able to both offer and receive empathy for the connection to be mutually beneficial. It isn't required to be empathetic, but it is crucial to be empathic regularly."

Empathy is not the same as agreeing with your feelings or having pity for them. Even if a person knows what you're going through, it doesn't always indicate that they agree with you or your reasoning. As an example, let's say you're upset and wounded by a friend's statement. While your partner may sympathise with your feelings of anger and pain, your friend's statement may not have been insensitive, even if it looked to be so to you. Countless conflicts and disputes had occurred due to the idea that empathy equalled agreement when one person grew enraged because she believed that if her partner loved her and knew how she felt, he would agree with her.

## A good mix of fun and responsibility

Fun and playfulness are essential components of every healthy relationship. But unless both participants in an intimate relationship take responsibility for their actions, one person needs to carry all or most of the blame. In this circumstance, one person is focused on play and enjoyment, while the other constantly attempts to convince him to understand and embrace his duties. This may lead to unfavourable sentiments between the two people.

Having fun and playing may bring out a child's curiosity and lovable features. Both of you want the other to have fun and engage in their interpretation of the play.

Adult duties may be daunting at times, and you may wish that you had less of them or that you could take a break for a few days or weeks. Even if you complain about your duties, you'll probably continue to do your best to fulfil them. Consider the person you're now seeing or married to. Is it generally true that this individual fulfils their responsibilities? Is that individual more concerned with having fun, having a good time, and the like? If the latter is true, enjoyment and play are not balanced by responsibilities.

## Positive emotional outbursts

It might be difficult to figure out how they feel when you're close to the individual since feelings and experiences can sometimes be obscured or concealed. An important characteristic of healthy relationships is the willingness of both parties to express themselves emotionally in a way that the other person may feel the effects of their actions. Neither of these is a waste of time since the other person may not be able to hear or comprehend what you're saying if you don't express yourself.

Some individuals have difficulties expressing their feelings freely because of early family-of-origin experiences in which open communication was discouraged or not encouraged at all. In addition, some individuals have been injured or disregarded when they expressed their sentiments. Others cannot communicate even the mildest of emotions, such as displeasure, and only do so in an improper manner when they are severe. You or your partner may fit into one or more of these categories.

## Begin the process of forgiveness

To create a new and improved version of yourself, it is necessary to let go of things that drain your resources (such as energy, time, and creativity) and are not helpful. Get rid of resentments and grudges as part of creating a relationship. Think of it as a productive versus a destructive duality. You may have to demolish something to construct something new. Some of your inner core self may need to be destroyed to establish your ideal self. Therefore you are urged to build a new version of yourself.

It's possible that you started reading this book with bitterness against your toxic parent because of the early and constant narcissistic wounds you suffered. Even though you now have a better grasp on how your parent's actions affected your self-esteem and relationships in subtle and unnoticeable ways, this does not indicate that you are ready to forgive and forget.

## Forgiveness

I'm often asked whether or not a child of a selfish parent should or must forgive that parent, and my response is always the same: no. At some point, forgiveness is feasible, but it's not a need. Rather than focusing on the negative consequences of their childhood, they could use their time and energy to develop their underdeveloped narcissism and form meaningful connections with others.

There is a clear and physical sense of relief, and people tell me how terrible it was because they could not forgive. Forgiveness may be attainable later when they've done enough inner work and introspection to make it feasible. As an outsider, it's much simpler to advocate forgiveness since you haven't had to deal with the daily or continual attacks on yourself by the self-absorbed parent, often continuing these assaults. Attacks on the adult child's self must be dealt with for forgiveness to be possible. The self of an adult child must be strengthened, developed, and validated to survive these assaults. Remember that even as an adult, your parent probably still feels and thinks all of the following:

- I made the proper decision.
- I had every right to act the way I did.
- It is immoral and disgusting for the child to question my behaviour, desires, and demands.
- My child would be grateful to me if they were worthy.
- I should be rewarded.
- My child would be a wreck if it weren't for me.
- I am more knowledgeable about my child's requirements than she is.
- My child is very sensitive and responds negatively to my helpful (in actuality, damaging) words.
- Regardless matter what I did, I always did it for her benefit.
- The child owes me a lot.

These self-absorbed parental attitudes might cause a person to relieve some of the bad sensations that may have been there since childhood. Looking through these difficulties and recognising the parent's feelings of despair, anxiety, and loneliness is likewise a difficult and unusual feat. They may have a lot of good things, but instead, they have nothing and have no idea how to make their lives better. The self-absorbed parent lacks the inner resources needed to enrich your life.

The profound emotional links between parent and child might hinder the adult child from being objective and entirely rational about a self-absorbed parent so that the parent's bad acts, statements, and answers can continue to harm. This makes it tough to forgive, if not impossible, to do otherwise.

Rather than forcing yourself to forgive because you've heard it's a good idea from others, you could find it more beneficial as an adult to put forgiveness on the back burner for the time being and instead concentrate on some intermediate actions that aid your recovery. Let's see if we can see any signs of healing that would indicate the need for interim measures.

If you think about your parent, you may come to terms with the fact that he or she is unlikely to change and that you have no great desire for him or her to do so. It's conceivable for a parent to change, but you recognise that you can't make them change.

Parents' critical, insulting, and degrading remarks don't hurt as much and have a shorter-lasting effect on you. These remarks still have the power to hurt, but that power is waning.

When it comes to your self-absorbed parent, you may still fear these encounters, but you don't leave them as churned up as you did previously; the repercussions of these contacts don't stay as long, and you may be more detached throughout them. You're also better able to control and regulate your emotions.

You are more aware of the potential for your feelings toward your parent to be transferred to others, and you attempt to prevent this from occurring.

Your most essential connections have improved due to your greater ability to empathise.

A more grounded and focused person does not react to the parent in a submissive or rebellious manner. You're also more conscious of when you're mimicking your parent's behaviour or reactions to others.

Eventually, you understand that you can stop your parent from hurting you as much and pick a more measured, less cruel reaction to the self-absorbed parent who does not disrespect either of you.

You get a lot in return from your other connections for the time, effort, and energy you put into them.

A profound connection may be formed between you and others in your most personal interactions when you can experience their sentiments without being entangled or overwhelmed.

At that point, you may go on to the next step. It's perfectly OK if you never get to this stage, and it's not anything to be ashamed of. There's no need to feel bad about yourself if you can't forgive. Before you can forgive, you must first be able to heal.

However, you have only just begun healing your core self, strengthening yourself against narcissistic damage, and letting go of the unfinished business haunting you for so long. Only you can complete this task. You've got the ability, and the skill can be developed.

## Conclusion

Your journey to discover the truth about yourself and the essence of existence is now complete. Is it easier to see where you're going? In other words, can you now picture life as a collaborative endeavour rather than as a stern toxic parent ordering you what to do? If that's the case, we've had a good time. The investment was worthwhile as soon as you began to take your well-being seriously.

Your life and your relationships will be better off if you care about your well-being and what happens to you in the world. Evidence shows that we perform better when we stop focusing on being excellent and instead focus on having fun. With any luck, you've gained a newfound appreciation for who you are, without the urge to change who you are into something you're not. Be who you are, and don't worry about pleasing anybody else.

Your sense of possibilities might awaken when you begin to treat yourself kindheartedly and empathically, with the enthusiasm of the sensitive parent who didn't exist in your life. Your most valuable resource is you, the sum of everything kindness and the absence of anything unimportant. Just go with the flow and go with your gut. The days of proving your value via self-sacrifice are finished, so stop listening to anybody who tells you otherwise. Trust that life will reveal what is important. You may rely on your life force to determine what is best for you. Your life will make sense if you align yourself with this mentality.

When you take control of your own life, you won't be able to be taken advantage of by anybody else. I hope this book of insights will continue to provide you with the inspiration you need to live an authentic life free of toxicity that is beneficial for you and the world. Remember to take care of yourself because you're worth it! All of these options are available to you. You don't have to live in a world filled with lies, deception, and other damaging tactics your toxic family has used against you. You have the power to get rid of them. This is something I've done. And there are many more who have done the same. You can do what we've done.

## Feedback

Thank you for reading 'How To Heal From Toxic Parents.' I sincerely hope you enjoyed and got value from this book, and that it helps you to forge those all-important positive habits that will bring peace and harmony to your life from this moment on.

If you have a free moment, please leave me some feedback on Amazon.

Also, scan the QR code below to visit the Hackney and jones Publishing website where you can find more information on the range of books available.

HackneyandJones.com

www.ingramcontent.com/pod-product-compliance
Lightning Source LLC
Chambersburg PA
CBHW031546080526
44588CB00018B/2715